Inside Out

A Journey to Inner Peace

Kim Babcock

BALBOA.
PRESS

A DIVISION OF HAY HOUSE

Balboa Press books may be ordered through booksellers or by contacting:

Balboa Press
A Division of Hay House
1663 Liberty Drive
Bloomington, IN 47403
www.balboapress.com
1 (877) 407-4847

Print information available on the last page.

ISBN: 978-1-5043-7886-4 (sc)
ISBN: 978-1-5043-7888-8 (hc)
ISBN: 978-1-5043-7887-1 (e)

Library of Congress Control Number: 2017905543

Balboa Press rev. date: 05/13/2017

Contents

To my family

Acknowledgments

My parents have always been my biggest cheerleaders, even when I wasn't encouraging myself. Mom and Dad, you've always showed me new ways to believe in myself, and your unwavering guidance has led me right up to this very moment. You've taught me to never settle for less than my best, and you've supported me even when I wasn't at my best. In every place I gave up or quit on myself, these were the very areas I always found you both, waiting for me with open arms and words of inspiration and motivation. Thank you for loving me every way you have. Your guidance echoes in my heart every single day of my life. You've always gone above and beyond. And to my sister Tiffany, you always leave me inspired to dream bigger and fly higher. You've been my sounding board through so much. You've taught me to forget all the fears and doubts and just go for it.

To my husband, Brian, the changes I've made personally and professionally have pulled you far beyond your comfort zone, yet you continue to love me. You've left your heart open for me, always offering your love and support, even when you didn't understand my journey. Thank you for your loving support. I am truly grateful to you, far beyond what words could encompass. From day one, I've always admired your hard work, ethics, and diligence. You've taught me so much about love and life that both will return to you what you've invested. You've given our family a beautiful life through hard work, sweat, blood, and tears. I wouldn't be here if it weren't for you. Thank you.

To my dear friends, Lisa and Maggie, both of you have inspired me through your strength and devotion. The depths of our friendship can never be measured. On some days, we've laughed ourselves right into delirium, and it was perfect. You both have always encouraged me to just be myself and have inspired me to chase my dreams. Lisa, you have given me strength I didn't know I had, and Maggie, you keep me grounded to always know who I am. Without a shadow of doubt, I know that, no matter what life throws at me, you both are always in my corner. Thank you. I thank God for putting you both in my life at the same time. Every time I think of you both, I smile. I am blessed by you.

To my clients, you are my heartbeat and the reason I have purpose. You are the driving force that motivates me every day. The reflection of truth in your eyes and the raw exposure of your heart that you've offered me brings me to my knees with humility. Tears well up in my eyes as I recall the thousands of sessions I've done with all walks of life, and yet the one common thread among you all is your beautiful, unwavering trust. The way you have faith in me drives me to be better each and every day. The sincere trust, honesty, and innocence in your eyes has unveiled a newfound joy and hope within me. The way you share your hearts, your stories, and your lives has humbled me to my knees and taught me more than I could ever thank you for. Each one of you has had a profound imprint on my development and me. You've taught me what resiliency looks like. Words can never capture the way you move me. I would not be here if it weren't for your open hearts. You've continually showed love and support and have allowed me to show you how amazing you truly are.

Above all, you've taught me how beautiful diversity is. I find new life, hope, and joy here. Thank you for inspiring me. I carry your smiles, laughter, tears, hugs, jokes, and friendships in my heart daily. I hope you all continue to dance to the beat of your own drum as you allow yourselves to become an instrument of the universe.

All photo credits and deep gratitude offered to PJ Brown, with Life in Rewind Films. Thank you for your hard work and trusting something new!

Exterior cover design credits to Caesar Augustus. Thank you for your love, and generosity in the hard work that you do! My gratitude to you is immeasurable.

Chapter 1

The Catalyst

Getting to know yourself in this day and age seems like a never-ending process. Everything in life continually changes. From one trend to the next, transformation is inevitable, which perpetuates the cycle of life. As this world continually spins faster and as this change pushes you to the next level of yourself, getting tangled up in the whirlwind of it can seem inevitable. The important thing to remember is that, although we may feel powerless as the world changes, we always have control over our inner worlds, personal powers, and the changes we allow within us. It is up to us to keep our inner spaces sacred, and what a gift it is to know that we have that choice, that power actually.

As I sit here and begin writing this chapter to share the event that drastically changed everything for me, I am dumbfounded in the realization that it is exactly two years ago to this day that I had the experience I am going to share. This event was the catalyst for changing everything in my life for the better.

It was November 7, 2015. I was driving to work, like any other day. At that time in my life, the death grip that my reality had on me was suffocating my existence. I was living a double life as a medium and a clinical coordinator for a physical therapy and rehab facility. I wanted change, and I needed the universe to help me make it happen.

While driving to work, I began begging the universe to please change my path and to put me on my true path of spiritual work, an effort that was so fulfilling to me. I continued in a state of resistance and emotional despair. I was trying to avoid my current situation and my life, and I was longing for something I did not yet have.

While still driving to work, in my heart I began pleading with the universe to give me a sign and make it so obvious that I could not miss it. I wanted a sign that would restore hope within me. I thought to myself, *Please give me a sign that will put me on my spiritual path and make it so obvious I can't miss it.*

Those were my actual words from my heart to the universe. Boy, was I brave. I didn't even realize what I was asking for.

Nonetheless the universe answered right then and there. I got what I asked for, but it wasn't in the way I expected. The universe took me very literally, and the next thing I knew, I woke up with my airbags in my lap and smoke everywhere. I was completely disoriented. I felt like I was waking from a deep, prolonged sleep, one that lasted perhaps from a past life to this one.

Here I was, waking up from an accident in complete and utter disorientation. The smell of the airbags and the smoke rolling from under the hood of my car were extremely nauseating. My ears were painfully ringing, and it was like I'd been standing next to a twelve-gauge shotgun during fire. The silence and stillness in the aftermath of the crash was deafening. As I looked down, I noticed my seat belt was still buckled. But my body had been shoved forward and to the right, causing the seat belt to dig into my hip.

Shards of intense, burning pain began shooting down the back of the right side of my neck. The stinging in my right hand began to set in. The airbag had struck my hand, and my entire hand was numb and briefly paralyzed. My knees were aching, and I was feeling shooting pain up my thighs from hitting the dash, I assume. And my right ankle was throbbing and bleeding a little. It had gotten tangled up with the gas and brake pedals.

As I came to and tried to gather myself, it hit me. I had been in a bad wreck, and looking out over the hood, I knew I had totaled my new car. I seemed to have been immediately robbed of my orientation to myself, my memory, and my surroundings. But I was grateful for the pain because it centered my awareness. I quickly realized that I certainly wasn't going to work anytime soon. The universe answered me quite literally, right then and there.

Eventually the EMTs showed up and took me to the hospital. They began flooding me with the normal array of questions: How old are you? What's your birthdate? And so on.

To my surprise, I couldn't answer them. Recalling my age or birthday seemed like a memory that was buried somewhere deep inside me. No matter how hard I tried or how many times I thought about it, I couldn't remember. In this moment, I knew something was wrong and couldn't help but cry. *What the hell is going on?* I thought to myself.

I was angry and embarrassed, and I was strapped to a gurney in the back of an ambulance. In these moments, I felt like I had completely lost myself yet all the while still somehow knowing myself.

I was evaluated and diagnosed with a severe brain injury and concussion. I went through three months of speech therapy and cognitive rehabilitation. I experienced symptoms like debilitating hypersensitivity to sound, severe decrease in proprioceptive abilities, extreme dizziness and vertigo, and confusion and memory loss. I still occasionally suffer with bouts of vertigo, but it's much more manageable. Memory loss has also been a great struggle and can be incredibly humbling at times. I guess, in a situation like this, you truly realize how human you really are. Talk about a rude awakening.

Looking back now, I realize that the experience I went through was a direct reflection of my consciousness, of my need to escape the current reality I was experiencing. Little did I know, it would become the catalyst and doorway to my awakening and complete self-awareness.

You see, in the time I spent recovering, I could not return to work. The good news was that I had already been practicing private readings and doing sessions on the side for a few years. And having had that practice under my belt, one thing I knew for sure was that I didn't need my human mind to function for me to channel and connect to the spirit world. It was my small glimmer of hope that maybe it really was time for a life change. I knew that, when I do my mediumship, I must suppress my mind completely anyway to achieve that connection. So, the fact that my cognitive function wasn't up to par seemed less of a threat, and while I was home recovering, I was elated to realize that I could continue mediumship. And so I did.

In the meantime, the company I worked for had lost its contract with the nursing home. The entire therapy department was dissolved, so I couldn't have returned to work even if I wanted to. This was the universe taking me literally and manifesting what I had asked for specifically. The news of my company losing the contract was perhaps one of the biggest motivators for me to just dive into my spiritual practice completely. I gave myself permission and took the leap of faith.

Within just a few months, I opened a local metaphysical shop where I practiced my readings as a medium and Reiki- a form on energy healing. I also held community gatherings for guided meditations. I maintained my shop for a year, and the response I received in my tiny little village of New Concord, Ohio, inspired me. In the time I spent at my shop and interacting with my clients and the community, I realized that people are spiritually starving and craving something more, something much bigger. While working in my community and even while on tour, I've identified a deep desire among people to know their spiritual selves. Individuals are longing to get to know their spiritual selves and to figure out what resonates with them. They desire a truer sense of self-identity.

I interacted with young children, college kids, high school students, adults, and even the elderly at my shop. No matter the age, I quickly realized that people are seeking something greater. They are searching for the deep connection to themselves, a link that bridges the gap between this life and the afterlife. They yearn for something that resonates deep within them and awakens their soul with a sense of fulfillment.

That collection of experiences produced the title of this book. I quickly recognized a population of individuals on the rise who are searching for spiritual depth and fulfillment. So many have turned themselves inside out in search for meaning and that true connection to themselves, the exploration of getting to know oneself beyond what they've been conditioned to know and believe.

Spirituality can easily become a fashionable term used to decorate the ego. I naturally felt compelled to help individuals turn their eyes back to themselves as they yearn to become more spiritually cognizant of their truth. I've encountered people who only had a sense of identity with external material things, and worse yet, I know many people who are addicted to their illnesses for a sense of identity. And through that addiction, they become divorced from their true identities.

All of these interactions fueled me even further to know what people are actually looking for. In 2016, I launched my first tour and traveled around the United States to host spiritual conventions. I traveled to six different cities: Honolulu, Denver, Sedona, Chicago, New York, and more. Throughout these travels as a medium, I found myself doing spiritual coaching instead of mediumship. So many different walks of life come to these events and search for something they feel a connection to.

And what I found after the tour is that, as a collective, the majority of mankind is living inside out. They are living inside out in the quest to know themselves, in their quest to find happiness and in their pursuit to know their purposes. As long as individuals believe they have to search, they have not yet realized what happiness is. It is not something to be found; rather it is something to be realized.

From as early as I can remember, I've always trusted the way I feel, and having faith in that internal notion has been my inner compass for growth and development. If something didn't feel right, I simply wouldn't associate myself with it, yet at the same time, I'd push myself through personal boundaries so I could continue to evolve. Many would call it stepping outside of my comfort zone. Although it might have been scary, I knew it felt right and resonated at some level deep inside.

Curiosity seems to pave the way for most of my self-exploration and personal growth too. I follow that curiosity through new depths of my soul, continually discovering myself in new ways. Customarily, others don't comprehend my actions, but I'm happy to be misunderstood. True freedom is personal development beyond the acceptance of others.

Strangely, I feel comfortable when I'm in a foreign place speaking with strangers. Perhaps it's because I uphold an everlasting adoration for all diversities in life. Perhaps it's because

I trust in something greater than myself and know my place inside that greatness. I have a love for breathing the air of new places and meeting new faces. I seem to find myself there. I love and appreciate all cultural diversities and can see how they all contribute to the collective evolution of humankind. I know and feel the truth in this now, but that hasn't always been the case.

Growing up, my high school years were some of the most difficult years of my life for many reasons. From my freshman year to my senior year in high school, instead of learning about life one sip at a time, I felt like I was drinking from a fire hose on full blast. As a freshman, I began dating (and am now married to) my high school sweetheart. He graduated and joined the military, and we soon began a long-distance relationship. I also began a promising modeling career but seemed to have lost all of my friends in that process.

As I recall this time in my life, I can count numerous occasions where I had to sometimes disarm my friends from their own jealousy and insecurities just to maintain a friendship. The trouble with this was that I would disarm them by humiliating myself. I've always been comfortable in my own skin and never felt the need to compare that to others. But when I could sense jealousy or see displays of inferiority among my peers, I would quickly do whatever I could to comfort them at their level of insecurity, and oftentimes that was at my own expense, especially when I shared the news of the modeling contract with my friends.

I quickly learned that, even with a modeling contract on the table in Miami, this career didn't feel right to me. There was a sense of emptiness with it. I have a great appreciation for models of all kinds because I've been there, but a good friend opened my eyes to the emptiness when she asked, "So how do you like getting paid to look pretty?"

At that moment, it was simple. It just wasn't me. I knew I needed more—more one-on-one connection with people and more opportunity to talk with new people and get to know their innermost thoughts. Modeling couldn't fill that void for me. I needed multidimensional connections that fostered love, authenticity, and growth.

In the years following high school, I went through what felt like a cyclone of circumstances—from getting married to becoming a mother and searching for my life's purpose and every step in between. I even dropped out of college five times before I finished my two degrees. I can say that now without embarrassment because I accept myself completely and understand that every level of my past has brought me to this very moment.

I searched externally for many years for self-definition but always seemed to come up empty-handed or unfulfilled. When I finally accomplished a degree in physical therapy and a bachelor of arts degree in health care management, I became a clinical coordinator for a rehab clinic at a local nursing home, providing physical therapy while managing the therapy clinic. I thought I had found my purpose, only to soon realize I'd feel unappeased once again. I settled into this role for a short time before I would begin the search, yet again.

I tried to fit into the normal routine that seemed most accepted by society, punching a time clock, setting up a 401(k), and creating a retirement plan. But again, something just did not feel right. I felt like I was living a lie, and when I had that feeling, I knew it was time to prepare for another change.

Trust in something greater than yourself, but

know your place within that greatness.

Chapter 2

Accepting Me

Throughout my life, I've personally battled with identity issues and truly knowing myself at the core level. I've witnessed my identity—or what I thought was my identity—collapse through different circumstances in my life. And now as I approach my mid-thirties, I know why my sense of identity didn't uphold in those circumstances. It doesn't exist there. But I'd have to go through many struggles to realize this.

One of the earliest examples I can remember is when I was probably in third grade. I rode the bus to and from school, and if you ever had to ride the bus, you know that what happens on the bus is far worse than what happens at school. Growing up, I was teased a lot. One boy in particular teased me daily on the bus. I was an easy target, I guess. He teased me about the mole on my face above my lip. My mom used to tell me that it was a beauty mark. So when the boys on the bus would tease me and ask me what was on my face. I'd tell them it was a beauty mark.

Their response crushed me, "Well, it sure isn't working."

When I got home from school that day, I actually picked the mole off my face. Their cruelty so mortified me that I tried to change the way I looked. Disgusting, I know. Even worse, the mole came right back. I had to accept it and ignore their cruel remarks.

As I grew and matured, not only was my identity changing, but so was the way I perceived the world. I went through numerous experiences that seemed to be solely based on my identity, and going through these different events made me fight even harder to get to know myself.

One example I can remember perfectly, when I was a new grad, fresh out of college from physical therapy studies, I had taken a position at an outpatient facility as a PTA (physical therapist's assistant). I was the only PTA at this chiropractic clinic, and made my own schedule. The chiropractor who hired me was rather young too. Now, being raised an Army brat, I was always taught that, if you're going to do something, you'd better give it your all or don't do it at all. And as a new grad in a new position,

I was intense about following laws and regulations that governed my therapy license. Shouldn't we all be anyways? I guess I was naïve in believing everyone was as law-abiding and ethical. When something was immoral, believe me, I didn't hesitate to knock on my boss' door and demand his time for a discussion.

I'll never forget one day in particular when I did this. I had the Ohio State laws memorized, and as I recited them to him and shoved his work back to him in disapproval of his immoral actions (mind you, he was my boss and a chiropractor), he was taken aback with my bravery and diligence. He sat back with his arms crossed, smiling.

I asked him, "Why are you smiling?"

"Ya know, Kim, I almost didn't hire you because you're pretty, and pretty don't work hard. But you impress me."

I didn't know what to think when he said that. Mostly, I was angry at such a surface level response.

On another occasion, before I had completed my therapy degree, I applied for a receptionist/bookkeeping position at a local medical aesthetics spa and got the job. When I was hired, I was blonde and thin. Months later, my husband and I were expecting our first child, and my thin figure was nowhere in sight. Also, I had colored my hair brunette.

One day, while at work, I was unexpectedly pulled into my boss's office. He sat me down and began to fumble around his words. Something didn't feel right, and I intuitively knew what was coming.

He finally spit it out, "Kim, when we hired you, we did so because you had a youthful appearance and thought you'd be a great face for our company. We are selling beauty, and we need that to be the first thing people see when they come in here. Now that your looks have changed, we don't think you're right for the position."

Yet again, I was furious. I knew this was illegal, but wouldn't you know? He also happened to also be an attorney. I left in tears and never looked back.

Situations like these in my life have always forced me to dig deep within myself. As I did, I was somehow always able to trust my inner self, knowing this was just a phase that would pass and lead me to something much better. I always fell back to that notion that, when one door closes, another is opening.

Many occasions like this throughout my life have dropped me at the doorstep of my true worth, and I'm grateful because I know now that my worth has nothing to do with my looks or my job. Whether my looks helped or hindered me, I've come to know that external, cosmetic parameters cannot capture my identity. It resides much deeper.

I've come to know myself in others too. Many times I've surrendered my comfort zone in an effort to grow. I appreciate the diversities among humankind and can easily find myself amid the diversities.

Circumstance could no longer uphold my identity, and as I came to know this, I released my grip on trying to make that happen. I've realized that my character will always speak for itself from the inside out and that anything external cannot encompass authenticity.

In growing to get to know myself, I also had a collection of paranormal experiences that I somehow knew were contributing to my identity as well. Throughout my childhood and early adulthood, paranormal activity was a normal experience for me. It wasn't something that really scared me; rather it inspired curiosity. Countless experiences from seeing spirit faces in my room, having electronics turn themselves on/off near me, and watching doors opening and closing nearby all inspired a deeper curiosity. As I grew curious though, I never shared with anyone what I was experiencing because I wasn't sure they'd understand. Only my closest friends knew of some of the experiences. The rest I kept private and hidden, like forbidden secrets of urban legends.

I felt like I was living a double life and began to know this state of reality very well. It was difficult and sickening. You see, throughout my childhood and even more so in my adulthood, I've always paid great attention to the nonphysical things. I could see people who weren't in the physical form, and soon I began to hear them as well. From my early childhood, I remember seeing faces on the ceiling in my room, not knowing who they were but not being scared of them either. I often heard inner guidance that proved to be extremely helpful in many difficult situations. This offered a level of comfort. As I grew older, I continued to experience paranormal activity in many ways, and it only seemed to grow stronger as the years rushed by.

Eventually, living a double life caught up to me and proved to be more than I could handle. Wrestling with both sides of myself was such a conflict of interest and certainly was counterintuitive.

Hiding one side of myself to give life to the other was debilitating and senseless. It was fatiguing to always live in fear. Eventually, I surrendered the battle, the double life, and allowed myself to become everything I was. Instead of trying to juggle them and balance both, I allowed both.

I realized that I no longer had to hide one to be the other, the medium versus the mother and wife. That was an illusion, a heavy burden, based in fear that I began carrying like a load of bricks on my shoulders. I no longer forced myself to change to comfort others. Giving myself permission to be true to myself was—and still is—the most freeing thing I could do for myself. The obstacles I've removed in my life by simply saying yes to myself have provided immeasurable growth.

In the years that I managed the therapy clinic, I became aware of my thoughts and how they made me feel. Further I also became cognizant that I was choosing to feel this way when I thought about work. It wasn't pleasant. Each day that I continued my work as a therapist, I felt myself moving further away from my own heart and my passion. My love for and passion in my spiritual work strengthened daily. My mediumship was growing stronger, and knowing my spiritual self, became the most fulfilling experience I'd been through.

In fact, I had one-on-one readings with nearly every one of my coworkers, my boss, and even the kitchen staff at the nursing home where I managed the therapy clinic. I let spirit guide me, and soon it became nearly impossible for me to focus on my job as a therapist. I still found myself confused and almost embarrassed of what was happening. My world seemed divided, and the sense of me that I was familiar with was changing drastically. I knew I didn't feel aligned, and something deep inside didn't feel right. I was torn and miserable.

As I continued working at the nursing home and became more aware of my abilities, I would have premonitions of events with my patients involved. I would see flash images of them falling, breaking a hip, or something worse. When these events came to fruition, the reality set in, and conflict with the ego did too. I began to blame myself because I thought, *Well, I saw that happen, but I didn't do anything to prevent it?*

Carrying that blame was painful. I remember walking past one of my patient's rooms down a hall of the nursing home and hearing in my head, "Today's her last day." I still get chills upon recalling that message because, later that day, that guidance proved to be correct. Hearing and seeing this type of information was not only fatiguing but confusing.

I argued many times, "Why me? Why am I hearing this? And what the heck am I supposed to do with it?"

I was too ego-stricken in the question to hear that answer at that point in time, but the events continued. The more frequent these events became, the more I began to recognize when I was in that level of awareness, to align with it and become the channel of spirit communication.

I'll never forget one day in particular. I came into work like any other day. I punched the time clock and turned the corner on my way to the therapy room. As soon as I did, spirit stopped me in my tracks and fixed my eyesight on a gentleman down the hall, to my left.

(At this point, I've come to realize that when I fix my eyesight on someone, there's a message for that person from spirit. When they grab my attention, everything becomes silent. I get tunnel vision, and my heart feels very still. Then the information flows in.)

So I briefly made the connection, listened, and continued to the therapy room. When a connection like this happens, I feel a sense of duty to deliver the message, but not knowing the person on the receiving end and not knowing how he will receive the message can make for some sickening anxiety.

I struggled terribly to get through my morning routine in the therapy clinic because the message for this man became stronger and louder as time went on. The energy was so intense that I felt like I was having an anxiety attack, but I knew this was the high vibration of spirit. I was breaking out in hot flashes and pacing the therapy room, trying to build up the courage to approach this man. I was still very nervous to approach a stranger with this. And besides, this man was there to install security cameras throughout the facility, not receive a message from a medium. But the energy continued, and after three hours of pacing, I finally mustered up the courage to approach him. I'm glad I did.

I shared with him what I saw and heard. A blonde woman came through at his side. She came through his heart, so I knew this was a significant other. She showed me a motorcycle and said, "Forgive yourself."

She continued with other validating facts to prove her presence and her peace. You see, seven years prior, this man had been in a motorcycle accident with his wife. He survived, but sadly she did not. Their daughter was only six weeks old at the time her mother passed in the accident. His wife came through with beautiful messages of validation that assured him that she was at peace. The messages also helped him to heal and forgive himself for the accident. Imagine a grown man on a ladder trying to install security cameras, now in tears after hearing messages from his departed wife through a perfect stranger. It was beautiful, encouraging, and healing. I felt so relieved after passing along the message.

Through experiences like this, it encourages me to deliver the unexpected messages from spirit. And the more I honored these occurrences, the more they happened. My entire paradigm began to shift. I was a closet medium, living my journey from the inside out.

Looking back, I've always been a person of a somewhat neutral disposition. I was able to easily detach from situations, people, and my own expectations. This level of detachment certainly helped when my entire world began to change and everything that once was my normal became foreign and expired.

I can honestly say that, as I embraced the change completely and surrendered the double life, I came into a sense of me that felt right, more complete than ever before. I quickly caught on that, when I do this type of work and stop resisting it, it takes me to a place of nirvana every time. When I truly honor myself, and be myself without any parameters at all, I would come to know the divine within. I guess this is how I realized that I had aligned with my true self, my purpose. It left me feeling like the most authentic 'me' I've ever felt. In knowing this and allowing it, I knew change was coming. I could feel the shift within, and it was only a matter of time before I experienced it on the outside too.

Giving myself permission to be myself is the

most freeing thing I've ever done.

Chapter 3

More than Medium

As a medium, coming out of the closet about my abilities in my late twenties was not an easy feat. After struggling for years, living a double life, and keeping my mediumship hidden, I'd finally realized that I couldn't live like this forever.

All my life, I've experienced paranormal activity, and in my late teens and early twenties, my mom was even into paranormal investigation as a hobby. Go figure. However, our worlds with paranormal activity and paranormal interest never did collide. I didn't understand the activity surrounding me until I researched it on my own. In my mid-twenties, I began clairvoyantly seeing book titles. Not knowing what else to do about what I was seeing, I would Google the title names. When the search results would pull up various books, I'd order them and highly anticipate their arrival.

I began reading about metaphysics and quantum physics, and the deep resonation with the contents of each book pulled me in further and helped me to understand what I was experiencing. The more I would acknowledge what I saw, the more I'd see. The books left me thirsty for more knowledge about spirituality, the afterlife, and metaphysics. It wasn't until I actually combined the material that I was reading with what I was experiencing that my thirst would be partially quenched. I say "partially quenched" because I work hard to keep space open in my heart for further growth and inspiration.

As I began to sort through different books, this information helped me to put structure to what I was experiencing so I could be productive with it. I began to get very comfortable with and started doing private readings on the side for individuals, all while still working in physical therapy, managing a clinic. The duality of these interests began to set in as the years passed by and seemed to be suffocating my joy. I was so unhappy working in health care, yet my mediumship was still a huge skeleton in the closet at the time.

I was raised Catholic and married a Catholic. Performing mediumship is viewed as evil witchcraft and unacceptable. In turn, I began living a double life, as I mentioned earlier. I'd kept my mediumship abilities private and had been hiding it from some friends and family for years. I was afraid of rejection and losing friends, but hiding my true self was painful, to say the least.

So many times in the past, when people would ask me what I do for a living, I would respond and say physical therapy, and simultaneously, my inner voice would say I was a medium. Living this dualistic reality was frustrating, saddening, and self-defeating. My inner voice wanted so badly to scream about my true passion in mediumship and share it with the world. I wanted desperately to share it with everyone I knew, and that enthusiasm festered inside of me.

As I look back on those years, I know now that I simply was choosing to hide that side of myself because of my own ignorant fear. When I finally realized I didn't have to hide my true self, my entire world changed for the better. I surrendered the fears of judgment, criticism, and vulnerability. I stopped living through others' expectations and became my true self.

Even as I came into my own, and allowed this shift in my life, abandoning my fear was not an easy process. It took time. I used to cringe when people would ask me what I do and I would have to answer and tell them that I was a medium. So many times, I wanted to say to them, "I'm more than a medium. Let me explain."

The word *medium* is a loaded word and comes with heavy responsibility and even heavier reactions. Oftentimes it'd turn people off, and the conversation would die quickly. I felt defeated before I even had a chance. If I did have the chance to explain, I knew I could open minds and hearts. I'd fumble to find the right, gentle words, with a giant nervous smile on my face. My voice would crack, and the sad puppy eyes would take over, hoping for at least the chance to be heard, to explain myself.

It's funny what fear can do. I'd get nervous and have myself all worked up. There have been times when I've received numerous funny looks and have been called some horrific names—a witch, a lunatic, a phony, and egocentric, to name a few. Some people have even shared that they're scared to be around me. And yet others have accused me of believing that I'm "holier than thou."

Despite the accusations and fear-driven, insecure remarks, at this point in my life, I've learned that what people say and do is only a reflection of their character, not mine. It feels good knowing this because it has repeatedly been my salvation from others' negative remarks. It takes me back to my childhood days when I used to think, *I'm rubber, and you're glue. What you say bounces off me and sticks to you.* Well, it's true.

If we choose not to allow any of these things to hurt us, it really does stay with the person who offered it in the first place. Knowing this, you'll always win and avoid feeling hurt. Others' ignorance to my profession isn't what hurts, and the names and comments don't harm me anymore either. They used to, but now I know better. What hurts the most though is the absence of open-mindedness. It sometimes breaks my heart to see individuals suffer the results of their own closed mind and hearts. Closed minds and closed hearts will always confuse me. I'll never understand it. Ultimately, I can accept it. I have to. I have no choice. I'm not in control of their consciousness. I just have to love them for where they are in their consciousness. Regardless, I know my truth, and I'll stand alone, if I must, to honor it.

It reminds me of Mark 13:13, "Everyone will hate you because of me, but the one who stands firm till the end will be saved." Personally, I know that many have hated me because I stand in oneness with God in my work, and I know my path there too. The route I choose to follow was given to me, not decided by me. But

I stand firm in it because, as I do, I'm already saved. No outward man can educate me on my relationship with God. This intimate relationship is only known through personal divine encounters and experience.

These people throwing stones at me, didn't even know why they were doing so. Typically, people criticize the things they do not understand to cover up their ignorance. The ego will often wear this mask. In criticizing me, they were simply expressing their fears. They saw that I had claimed my power in something, and in watching me, perhaps subconsciously, they were acknowledging their deficits.

Usually, defaulting to fear and criticism is what I see most people succumb to. Again, it isn't the ignorance that frustrates me. Not at all. I'm ignorant to many things, and actually I find it empowering to be able to admit that without shame. The unwillingness to be open to something new boggles my mind. I suppose though, that, when someone is ready to expand in his or her consciousness, he or she will open up and explore new things. Until then, I practice my capacity to accept what is, and often times that means accepting varying levels of consciousness.

When I'd tell people what I do, often, I would immediately see arms cross and eyebrows become angry. The judgment and skepticism grew strong in their eyes, and without them saying a word, I knew the door was closing on me, to share what I hold sacred in my heart.

Back in 2006 when I was in school for physical therapy, my best friend at the time, also in the same academic program, had lost her brother years prior. That was all I'd known. I'd never met him and didn't know my friend until seven years after his passing. I'll never forget sitting in class one day and seeing all sorts of images of this young man in my mind's eye.

This young man said he was my best friend's brother. He showed me what he was wearing and provided other details that would later validate his presence. I was very nervous and apprehensive to share this with my friend, but I did.

She was very skeptical, but open-minded. I explained to her what he looked like to me, and what he was wearing. She then showed me a picture of him, and it had indeed been the same young man I saw. Then, when I told her what he was wearing, her eyes welled up with tears as she told me that what I saw, was what he was buried in. I couldn't believe it! At this point, my mediumship was in it's infancy, but as I look back, I never hesitated to trust what I saw. I was very matter-of-fact with it and trusted the information I was given. Reading energy and vibrations is second nature to me these days, and reactions like these have become pretty common.

Those reactions only propelled me to share with people that I am a medium, but also more than a medium. I am a spiritual coach, a mother, an Army/farmer's wife, an Army brat, an auntie, and a sister. I have children who have nuclear meltdowns and good friends who are suicidal. I try as hard as I can to be the best I can at each of these, but sometimes I must be diligent about my own personal discernment.

I have a personal code of ethics too, that I lace into my mediumship practices. I've encountered many individuals who carry a strong sense of entitlement, and this has become the best place for me to exercise those ethics. Just because my client feels entitled to know something doesn't mean I'll channel that information. I often walk a very tight rope. I know my scope of practice as medium, and I recognize it very well. I'm always looking for opportunities to grow, but I will not ask something of myself that I simply don't resonate with. It's like asking a teacher to be a doctor for a day. Sometimes when I feel compelled to help, it's hard to say no. It's difficult to accept my own limitations, but what's even harder is forcing something I don't align with.

As I accepted my mediumship, I knew this was a path I would have to walk alone at times because it was such a drastic change from my prior lifestyle in health care, but sometimes standing alone was the most empowering position I could put myself in. I didn't need anyone's approval or justification of what I was doing.

The authenticity feels so real through my connection with God, and this was the way I came to know myself with God. This was—and still is—all the justification I'll ever need. It's something that man cannot touch or compare to. The way God speaks to me inside is mine, and no external thing can ever shake that. The power in that realization is what continues to push me forward each and every, day as a medium and spiritual coach.

On the contrary, other times when I share with people that I'm a medium, some individuals light up with curiosity. They ask a million questions, and then the spark inside them is ignited, to begin their quest for knowing themselves too, as a spiritually centered individual. It is a fine line, and each and every time someone asks me what I do for a living, I never know how that person will react. I've encountered individuals who shun what I do and others that dismiss the sacred value of it all together, and treat it like a party trick, like I'm a clown performing on demand at some sort of freak show. I love what I do, but when someone comes at me with a 'prove-it' attitude, I simply have to walk to the other way.

As a medium, I'm not here to prove anything; instead I'd rather teach you, how you too, can listen to your divine inner being, and connect with the spirit world. The common thread between us all is our spirit essence, a place that we all exist among. And as we take physical form, it is a mere shift in consciousness, to demonstrate, that consciousness itself exists in any and all forms.

You see, my goal here in sharing is to help you realize your inner divinity, that place inside you where the nirvana exists. As I have traveled around the United States and have shared my channelings publicly, as published in the *Sedona Journal of Emergence, Channeling Erik Blog,* and other blogs, I hold myself to very high standards. These next few paragraphs are the essence of this chapter and probably this entire book too. Stay with me.

Throughout life and amid the universe, we are always simultaneously a teacher and a student. I know I uphold space for both in my heart. In doing so, I have come to realize important concepts of both. As the teacher, we should always uphold a code of morals and ethics in the highest good of all concerned. As we do, our actions will reflect the same. Our actions are not singular; our thoughts are not limited to being only self-realized.

Believing so is a fatal mistake. It all begins at the level of our core, from the inside-out. We influence the world we live in and the universe as well. The essence of our being, the God presence in us all, is omnipresent, universal, everywhere, and infinite. Therein you too, are omnipresent in spirit and essence. Your thoughts and actions are omnipresent, and universal.

This reminds me of a powerful quote that I have often seen come to fruition, "Your beliefs become your thoughts. Your thoughts become your words. Your words become your actions. Your actions become your habits. Your habits become your values. Your values become your destiny."

In knowing this, whether we resonate more as a teacher or a student of the universe, we must stay grounded in realizing our responsibilities in both. If the teacher has no code of ethics, no morals, or no boundaries, then non-virtue will be transmitted. And if the student fails to value personal discernment amid the teacher's lessons, he or she too will fail to thrive in virtue. Both are responsible. Sadly, many are deceived by their own laziness though, and often blame the other when life lessons seem difficult.

As a medium and spiritual teacher, I've never felt obligated to channel messages, connect to spirit, or share my channelings. I do it because I love it, and share it if I believe it'll help. Another person's sense of entitlement will never overrule my personal discernment. I know the responsibility that my work carries, and I take that seriously.

As I mentioned earlier, I launched a tour in 2016, hosting spiritual conventions throughout the United States. Interacting with all of the guests at each event taught me so much about humanity. And as a medium, through me, my guides occasionally offer their guidance and advice as well, and we often team up at these events to provide direction through various workshops. Each workshop was geared toward spiritual growth and expanded consciousness, and was attuned to the collective consciousness of each individual group. I quickly found myself ascending beyond my mediumship abilities to provide spiritual coaching to those seeking something greater.

Adversely, I also had to continue to remind myself that I'm more than a medium, on numerous occasions, and others that my mediumship was not a party trick. I can recall many times where it was treated that way. In those times, I had to remind myself that this was simply something sacred to me and not to them, and as long as I kept reminding myself of that, somehow that kept them from affecting that sacred inner space. That simple self-reminder transmuted my desire to react negatively to the situation.

I came to realize that, the more I did this, the stronger my heart-centered awareness had become. I was simply taking time to slow down and connect to my heart, to that inner space of bliss that I keep referencing. Each time I did though, it became clear to me that a few very valuable things were happening here. First, simply by using my intentions to connect to my heart, I was nourishing my heart. The very action of taking time for it (my heart) was its nourishment. Also, I was able to clear my own thought debris and reconcile once again, between my head and my heart. This had become my daily practice, my meditation, if you will. It then became my mantra, "My heart is nourished; my heart is nourished."

As I utilized this mantra, thought debris was easily cleared, and it became easier to connect to heart-centered awareness. As I traveled, I took this mantra on the road with me as a bridge between vulnerability and change. When I'd arrive to a new place, vulnerability was required of me as change took place within me. Both can present a feeling of unease, yet, as long as I'd bridge the gap between the two, with heart-centered awareness, I knew I was okay.

While on tour, I often encountered individuals who asked me how they could be more like me. People would often refer to my mediumship abilities as a God-given gift. Although it would be quite pleasing to the ego to believe that, I know it's not true. My abilities are not a gift. It is kindly accepted as a compliment, but please know that I don't consider it a gift. When others do, especially in a self-righteous manner, my skin crawls. I cringe inside. Division is created among this belief. Mediumship, empathic, psychic, and spiritual intuitive abilities essentially all come from the same source—the very foundation that is within us all, the God source, a basis of divine oneness that we are all created in, from, and exist inside of. To me, I see it as a level of awareness that I've shifted my focus to and become conscious of.

It isn't a question if everyone has the same abilities, but it's rather the capacity to align with them. They are all abilities that I have simply aligned my consciousness with in order to exercise them. I have nothing different, more, or greater than anyone else. I've simply just shifted my awareness to something different. You can too.

In the world today, we are veiled with the conditions and expectations of society. Our actions are limited by, and even subject to these veils. Societal beliefs, fads, and cultural and religious traditions and expectations become our identity. When we can see past those conditions, we can remove the veils. Our ability to know ourselves without the veil creates unity among us all. Then true nirvana is realized, and freedom is experienced.

As we develop ourselves in this higher consciousness, we must realize how important it is to abandon the searching and striving for higher consciousness. As long as we are striving, searching, looking, or even forcing, we'll continue to experience the deficits. We must let go of all the externally imposed attachments, beliefs, and traditions. We must develop a new way of life that upholds internal value at the level self, the core level, and through personal experience, it upholds the capacity to continually observe self.

When individuals come up to me and ask how they can be more like me, quite honestly every time I hear this, my heart breaks a little. I know the pain and suffering of wanting to be like someone or something else, and it is an illusion that creates much suffering, division, and a longing that is never fulfilled. Deep down, I know the illusion that we're different or separate is what they were defaulting to in their level of consciousness, or lack thereof perhaps. I also know from experience that, as long as someone is seeking outside of himself or herself for happiness, fulfillment, joy, or pleasure, all those things will never be realized.

Perhaps the most difficult part of it for me was that the realization of one's beauty in one's own existence must be self-realized. If one is living inside out and searching the external, material world for that happiness and fulfillment, it can only be through self-realization that the search is reversed, and the individual looks inside for joy. It takes a deep level of emotional honesty and self-trust to dwell internally. Most people are uncomfortable dwelling internally, and we've turned into a nation that is hyper extroverted, -or inside out.

The realization of knowing that I can't make someone realize the beauty of who he or she is was a tough lesson to saturate.

I can only help an individual along that path to achieve that realization. In coming to that realization, perhaps that's also the inspiration in writing this book, to give individuals a tool to guide them along that path of self-realized divinity. I've encountered many individuals struggling with thoughts of suicide because these external searches have continually failed them. They have yet to be emotionally honest with themselves as to why they hate themselves or the world they live in. This was when I realized I'm more than a medium, and spiritual coaching began.

As I discuss spiritual coaching, I also view it as teaching, so I'll use the terms interchangeably. Through the years, I've come to realize that a great teacher does not fixate on specific lessons, and create an identity within those teachings. A great teacher does not forcefully impart knowledge to the student and expect the student to become like the lesson or, worse yet, like the teacher. Rather a great teacher opens minds and hearts; fosters the student's ability to become self-directed, self-reliant, and innovative without becoming self-righteous; creates unity in that, open hearts and minds foster acceptance and adaptability; and instills the ability to value experience as personal knowledge rather than utilizing logic. Personal experience is your truth, and your bank of wisdom. Logic is just logic; it is finite with no room for growth.

As a practicing medium and spiritual coach for over seven years now, I've tried to familiarize myself with metaphysical terminology and jargon without creating attachments to these labels and information. We are spiritual beings, bridging the gap between the physical and spiritual self. We must recognize that first, before we can effectively bridge the gap between the two, but perhaps the jargon loosely thrown around in our culture has actually become a hindrance to our growth, on a personal level.

I've seen many individuals over-identify with labels and titles, and, as a result, develop tunnel vision in their attachments to the jargon. Sadly, if we give life to the ego side of ourselves, bridging that gap will be difficult because ego deflects the truth and resides in its own illusions. With the New Age industry on the rise and so many people becoming interested in deeper, meaningful spirituality, and closinging the gap between spiritual and physical selves, I've seen more and more people who have been fooled by the illusions of the ego. This is exactly why I am writing this, in hopes to simply share my perspective on the differences.

You see, it is even difficult for me to call myself a medium because it is such a loaded label. In some ways, it gives life to the ego because it is a label. The ego has no existence without labels, good or bad. The essence of our being cannot be defined by any certain label and transcends through all the labels that the ego uses to define its existence. If we need to define ourselves in such a way, we haven't woken up yet to our true essence. These are all fallacies that the ego creates, and we'll talk more about that in the coming chapters.

True self-realization comes when we understand that the essence of our being cannot fully be captured using labels or external justifications. After years of practicing my mediumship, I soon realized this as well. And in those years, I have quickly realized that we are all mediums, psychics, and intuitives. We are all empaths and seers. And as spiritual beings, our essence exists far beyond those labels. If a psychic or intuitive tries to convince you that he or she has something special that you do not, you should hopefully realize, they too are in ego.

If it weren't for knowing my spiritual self, and recognizing that God is the host of my being, these abilities would have no home inside me, but because of my focus and attention, I developed these abilities. My devotion to it, has developed my strength in it. And since we all have a spirit body, we all can accomplish these connections too, far beyond what the word *"medium"* can capture. Our most natural state is our ethereal body, and at this level, telepathic communication and quantum interaction is the authentic true form for our interactions.

For xample, how many times have you been in a room that someone else enters, and without saying a word, you know he or she is in a bad mood? You likely realized this because it was communicated through clairsentience (feeling).

We've only come to adapt to our limitations based on our physical existence in what society has conditioned us to believe. My guides continually remind me that the only barriers in life are the ones you accept-self imposed.

As this world spins faster and becomes more dizzying at times, more and more people are searching for inner peace. The only trouble is, that they are searching through material things and allowing that inner peace to exist inside out, completely exposed to the external world and subject to false realities as a place of existence. This type of search will only continue to perpetuate the illusion and provide results of fleeting fulfillment.

The more I grew into my own shoes, the more I realized there's no true reference point that fully encompasses my being, or anyone else's for that matter. Shedding all those beliefs and conditional thoughts was a trying process. Soon I realized I was aligning with a higher consciousness of myself, ascending in my connection with God.

As I followed my inner guidance and allowed my old self to die, I quickly realized that, at some point or another, to stand true in my path, I might have to stand alone. And I did. With God as my host and driving my purpose to help others recognize this within themselves too, I'll stand alone if that's what it takes. I'm not afraid to stand alone because at least I know I'm staying true to my heart, nourishing my existence within God. Nothing has ever felt more authentic to me, and the divinity and sacredness of my being have been revealed to me in that process. That is something that the word "*medium*" cannot fully embody. My own sacred divinity with God has been revealed to me, and since then, I've come to realize the infinite possibilities in that bond. This was a miraculous and overwhelming experience, and realization. My goal is to help others realize the very same thing in themselves.

An external search for peace is an infinite quest.

Chapter 4

Inside Out

An external search for peace is an infinite quest. As long as we externalize the search, we'll always end up empty-handed. True peace and fulfillment occur on the inside, not inside out. Keeping the inner space sacred is an art these days, in a world that lives inside out. As I've said before, as long as you believe peace is something to search for, and find, you haven't quite awakened. Peace is a realization, an understanding of your existence at the core level, not something to find.

In a culture that extroverts almost everything, we quickly forget that we exist amid a universe that is all-in-one. The energetic exchange of anything is mutual. It seems that, as a culture, we've become used to turning ourselves inside out, offering our hearts on a chopping block, in an effort to find peace. We do this every time we extrovert our efforts to find peace. As long as we think peace and internal nirvana is something to find, rather than become, we'll be stuck inside an infinite quest to find it. This unconscious state of awareness creates a victim mentality, as most people believe that circumstances happen to them, rather than knowing that all experiences happen through them, and are a mere reflection of their level of consciousness and the reality they experience, is a manifestation of their thoughts.

A famous quote from Buddha transcends thousands of years, "Peace comes from within. Do not seek it without." This simple yet profound phrase can teach us so much, if we're willing to open our minds and do the work. The Buddha teaches us that the true peace, true bliss, and happiness can only be realized within. Peace and happiness reliant upon anything and everything external, is merely just an attachment. These attachments, disillusion us from our true self-awareness and, then create a dependency upon external things, ultimately leading to suffering.

The internal nirvana within us all is a place that only the self can realize. Nothing external can bring us to this state of awareness. No one else can realize it for us and shift our consciousness accordingly, yet sadly, every time we extrovert our efforts to find internal nirvana, that is the very expectation we are trying to fulfill, that someone else can do it for us. It is a matter of being and becoming, not a matter of searching and finding. If we rely on and dwell in our inner sacred space, we experience true bliss—uninterrupted, unwavering, unconditional, unequivocal, unmitigated, unquestionable, and unmistakable bliss. Need I go on? Hopefully you get my point. The internal nirvana within us all, does not have or need parameters. It is infinite, eternal, and immortal.

The outside world doesn't have your personal power. Only you do, and only you can realize it. That's why you exist. But in turning yourself inside out, looking outside yourself for that power, you give it away. In searching externally, we abandon our own self-worth and inner peace. Many of us have done this in relationships and even workplaces. We've let our happiness become contingent upon the health of a relationship or success at work. These attachments create stagnancy. And though these factors may greatly impact our lives, they have nothing to do with our inner bliss, our true place of peace that resides within us all.

Unfortunately, so many people still seek happiness on the outside, and in that external search, they perpetuate that state of unfulfillment. This quote from the Buddha is perhaps one of the most powerful quotes of all, yet our complex nature as humans often overthink it or even dismiss it. The teachings of the Buddha remain timeless in its relevance due to our inside-out nature as humans.

Amid that external search for peace and happiness, we dismiss the value of our own self-worth. We place higher relevance and value on something external rather than internal, therefore, living inside out. Our identity, happiness and fulfillment, and even entire existence become inside out. Living in this way, is experiencing hell through our own egos. Ego needs all things external to have existence and cannot possibly live in God's house, that inner sacred space in your heart. God did not create us and give us life to be victims of our own hell, through our punishing thoughts. And the moment we allow the external world to depict and determine our value and, our peace, we are experiencing our own hell created by our ego, turning ourselves inside out.

Nothing and no-one externally can teach you about, or make you realize your divinity with God. That is something that must be self-realized. When you introvert your efforts to find that divine being, you will then realize it cannot even be slightly affected by the external world unless you give it permission. As soon as you become the host and allow the external things in, that will skew your ability to align with your own divinity.

Often-times, as we search within our understanding, God's essence becomes punitive. The true essence of God, and His presence within us is not subject to our beliefs and understanding. God does not pick and choose who to love and who to abandon. His existence cannot be held within particular parameters, rules, and regulations. I fear, however, that many have fallen asleep in this belief. God's existence is not contingent upon our understanding, and God's love within us is not conditional, based upon the good we do. Why would God encourage our love to be unconditional, if that were the case?

Then too comes the realization that, if we can only be ourselves, per the likeness of those around us, then we do not yet know who we ever are. We only know who we are in the reflection of others.

God has an affinity for you, within you, and in all things, and by accepting that, you nourish the soul and contribute to your own higher conscious revolution. If your ability to accept that divinity within you, is dependent upon external circumstances, then you have not yet made complete contact with the God essence inside you. I remind you that, you need not make that contact at all, for God to be in you. God's essence is already—and always will be—there. God cannot abandon Himself inside you.

The title of this book and this chapter came to me after having many experiences with people of all kinds from all walks of life. I've seen so many individuals seek externally for happiness, joy, pleasure, fulfillment, validation, and so on, only to find these feelings and emotions continually escape them. Usually this is where our paths crossed, and I began to coach them as best I could.

I find it painfully interesting, that, as a culture, we diligently protect societal beliefs, traditions, trends, fads, ideations, and overall, all things that are collectively accepted. Perhaps, we are only protecting them because that was expected or what the rest of society does too. We protect and safeguard these things because, most times, we're upholding our identity within one of them. Sadly, though, we aren't protecting and enforcing that protection because of personal experience, but because of what is accepted and expected. We've turned ourselves inside out in knowing what our morals and values are, and instead, aggressively protecting external, societal ways.

My internal being, my inner place of peace, has always been my safe haven. From a very early age, I can remember sitting in my friend's front yard with her, in West Virginia on a hot, sunny day. We were pretending to be gymnasts, and exhausted from the heat, we decided to sit in the grass and take a break. As we did, I noticed that she seemed unhappy. I could tell something was bothering her, so I asked her what was wrong. Angry tears fell from her eyes, and she pushed her lips together. She explained feeling like her family was always unfair to her.

As she went on, I could tell this had been bothering her for some time. Her misery consumed her, and she explained that she was feeling invalid, like nobody was listening to her. I could see the pain she was in. I could empathically feel it, but I knew I didn't want it to consume me, like it was her. I must have been about eight years old or so at the time, and even then, I remember introverting back into that internal space, that place of peace, that always felt like me, like a safe home, no matter what.

Somehow, at this young age, I knew that anything external could not touch or affect my sense of self. I always knew I had this home inside me, my very own safe haven, that always had an open door. I could return anytime I needed to. As a child, it was like my very best hiding place.

As I look back over the years, I've always known this. I didn't come to understand it though, until my early adulthood. Now I know the key is to maintain awareness, from this safe place, all of the time. This internal dwelling place was always warm and welcoming and seemed to be able to comfort me, no matter what I was going through. I now know, this is my inner peace, God's place in me, or the divine inner being. At that young age, I knew I could go to this place, but I wasn't quite able to articulate what this place was or even understand why it was. I just simply accepted it and knew it was there.

I've carried a continual connection with that sacred inner dwelling spaced throughout my entire life. In a nation that has widely become externally reliant and focused, I value this inner dwelling space more now than ever. The peace that resides in this sacred space cannot be affected by anything external, and is not contingent upon any circumstances or conditions in order for its own peace to exist. This is the divine self, the affinity within us from God and by God. My spirit guides have helped me to understand this. This is what I call home. Home is God's presence inside our heart. This is the truest, purest version of ourselves. I believe this is why we say that, after we die, "We go back home." We're returning back to our purest state, the essence that has been in us the entire duration of our physical life, and there beyond too.

In my own personal side thoughts, perhaps that's why scripture says our bodies are a temple. In 1 Corinthians 3:16, it reads, "Don't you know that you yourselves are God's temple and that God's spirit dwells in your midst?" God has built His home, His presence, inside of each one of us. It's a pure and divine space for inner dwelling. Let this sink in and hopefully create unity, knowing our inner place of peace is perhaps the most common thread among us all.

Time and time again, as I revert back to my inner place of peace, the God essence dwelling inside me, I have achieved a higher understanding of who I am. When my emotions seem like they're governing my behavior and even my happiness, I realize I've left my home. I've disconnected from my divine self. Outside of the home is where I experienced the unhappiness that the ego has to offer. Practicing mindfulness will help us stay aligned with this divine higher self. As you come to realize the inner peace that exists inside you, your home, and how indestructible it is, you will also experience an incredible new level of freedom.

That's the affinity that God has placed in each of us. Some might have never visited their own home before, and their home may be a completely foreign feeling to them. But it surely doesn't mean that their home does not exist within them. Perhaps it simply means their consciousness has not aligned with their home yet; therefore, the lack of awareness creates the feeling of absence.

I've also met many people who know the home is there but don't have the key to enter. They feel lost and seek guidance to enter their sacred space. In a world that is so used to complexities and adversities, it is quite simple to align with this sacred space. In my experience, I've realized the simplicity of it, becomes the challenge for us to accept.

You see, this divine sacred space inside us all has nothing to do with anything that we know in this material world. It is pure, beyond, outside of, and in between all the things that create the material world. Your home is where your true consciousness resides, and ego cannot possibly simultaneously exist here. Ego needs circumstances to exist, and your home exists beyond circumstances. It is pure love. Your home's existence has no boundaries and, no limits of time and space, and that is all the ego will ever know. Because your home is boundless, that is why circumstances cannot be kept here. Imprints from the ego will always stain the external world, but the internal sacred home can never embody such an imprint because its mere existence is infinite. The stains, however, are finite. The divine source within us all is pure and cannot uphold these stains caused by the ego.

Sadly, I've met hundreds and hundreds of people who still define their inner space as tainted, corrupted, hurt, and not a place of peace. Essentially what they are experiencing is their emotional reactions to their circumstances or even expectations. Deep emotional honesty is required to navigate your way into the home. The more emotionally honest one can be with oneself, the more one will peel back layers of all emotional attachments and find the authentic self, residing beneath those layers, in the home.

Emotions are merely a way to express yourself, but they do not represent your true essence. Emotions, however, are important for personal growth. I view them as stepping-stones for development. This is not a bad thing. Emotions can help one navigate their way through grief or pain. You see, if one chooses to express his or her sadness or anger, that expression is the stepping-stone to the next level of one's self. Perhaps not having the choice to express emotions would leave us feeling powerless at times when we already feel hopeless. Expressing our emotions can help us to rehabilitate the very pieces of ourselves that we abandoned and became hopeless. As long as we don't unpack our bags and reside in that emotion, we'll continue to prevail through it.

As I mentioned, deep emotional honesty is required, but often people turn away from the truth if the truth hurts. You must be emotionally honest with yourself and assert your attachments before you can truly let go of them. If you're not truly ready to let go of the attachment, that's when you encounter the truth as pain. Whatever you are resisting, by resisting, you become it. The resistance, too, is an attachment. Shedding these layers can be quite liberating because, in the process, you too will realize how the basis of your existence and even definition of your personality has been contingent upon circumstances or conditions. In coming to the realization that, your happiness needs no circumstances to exist, the epiphany can be quite overwhelming.

Align with your sacred inner space, and you'll escape being enslaved to the ego for happiness and validation. Maintaining inner space for inspiration is key. If we've allowed that space to become crowded with expectations and emotional attachments, we'll soon become jaded with life. Allowing ourselves to be inspired rather than seek inspiration fosters fulfillment and personal evolution.

Others may not understand you or your dreams, but do you need them to know it's what you want? Of course not. Your heart already knows. Listen to your heart. Your heart knows what it wants, it's just you and your fear that hold it back. Take that leap of faith. Trust that life, and the universe will teach you what you need to know, and provide you with exactly what you need.

As I write this, recalling my time spent on the beautiful beaches of Oahu earlier his year, the thought crosses my mind of how symbolic the beach is in correlation to life. The sandy shores, represent humans and how we experience life. The waves represent life itself, never-ending changes. The waves crash upon the shore. Some are larger than others, much like the way life experiences can crash upon us. Some moments are more monumental than others. And as the waves keep coming in, unwavering in their effort to flirt with the sands of the shore, it reminds me of how life experiences keep flooding in, all in an effort to flirt with and awaken our consciousness. The waves of the magnificent ocean beg and plead with the sandy shore, occasionally taking bits and pieces from the shore back into its sea belly, as the wave dies down.

Similarly, some of our life experiences take us with them, in heart. Again, much like these life experiences, at times, some of the bigger waves in life can wash us away and claim our identity if we're not mindful. We can be like the sandy shore, persuaded by the waves of experience in life, but like the shore, though pieces of us get washed away, the strongest and perhaps the best part of us will always remain.

And in fact, it does. Our divine inner being and its essence is never persuaded by external things. The mind simply imposes the ideas that the heart is affected, and if we always believe our thoughts, we can fall into that illusion. Maintaining connection to your inner stillness, that doesn't become disrupted by any outside emotion, event, or person is higher self-consciousness. To put it in different terms, the most viable way to explain this is being able to see and observe yourself experiencing life, from a higher (but not separate) perspective (your higher self). It's like an out-of-body experience almost, watching yourself go through and experience life from, the perspective of your higher self.

However, within our basic selves, we employ various emotions, and give them life. We manifest a continuum of circumstances that reflect that level of awareness. Unconsciously, we are aligning with various emotional realities all the time, associated with our hopes and dreams or even our regrets, and in this process, we continually manifest these realities and suffer the stagnant cycles. These again, are cycles of the unconscious level of awareness. We then react to the experiences emotionally, and perpetuate the cycle, until we become conscious enough to realize that our reality is a direct reflection and manifestation of our thoughts. Most people, though, will avoid taking responsibility for this thought.

You aren't your thoughts, but you are what you think you are. And as we react emotionally to our thoughts, we bypass the sacred inner space all together. The sacred inner space does not need to engage and react to the thought process at all.

We repeatedly subject it to the external world for justification and validation, and in turn, the core of our being becomes bruised and unwell. We extrovert our search for love, peace, and joy, and as soon as we do, we've already surrendered self-love that resides in our sacred inner space and completes our existence. Pure, absolute self-love is not subject to the external world. It is not changed or altered by the external world and never needs it for validation or existence. You see, instead, it is through this love that everything exists.

People have overidentified with the external world, and its circumstances. A vast majority of mankind have become bona fide extroverts in their infinite quest for peace. It's the tangibility of the material world that we falsely and only temporarily achieve fulfillment through. We've become reliant on the teacher instead of relying on what's being taught, turning ourselves inside out. We rely on material things, people, and places to provide us a sense of peace, and although these things can foster peace, it is not the true source of it. As we extrovert our quest for peace and happiness, we'll continue to experience fleeting fulfillment.

You see, we are all spiritual beings—or rather beings of energy—which means we are all connected to a larger universal pool of information. But sadly, we are quick to dismiss our own inner connection to the universe and employ the physical functional self for quick results. Our sacred inner space becomes tainted and crowded once again. Maintaining its purity simply means knowing that it's essence is not affected by any circumstance, good or bad. Only when we allow it to be affected—or rather believe that it can be affected—do we fall away from it once again.

I once had a client ask me, "I feel so happy and at peace inside when I travel to places I love, but when I go home, it's different. How do I maintain this feeling?" I reminded him to uphold the sacred inner space with mindful awareness that nothing affects it unless you give it permission to. The wonderful feeling inside, where happiness resides, is a choice. As soon as we react negatively through our emotions, we've allowed it to become affected by the outside world. Then, if we seek validation from the material world, our sense of purpose is lost, and validation is elusive. At best, we'll feel like our heart is breaking down on us, as our sense of self becomes impaired and externally dependent, ultimately employing the ego and all its struggles.

The experience and existence of peace does not need emotions to know itself, and the essence of our being, and the sacredness of our inner space, does not need emotions to exist. The core of our being is not governed or defined by our emotions, but if we let it, we employ the unconscious state of awareness, and experience the pain and suffering associated with it. Emotions rely on circumstances for existence and expression. Our divine inner peace is constant, above and beyond all circumstances.

The most magnificent part of this is the realization that all emotions are a choice. Humans are the host, and if we choose to host certain emotions, we'll experience everything on that same level vibrationally, as that emotion. If we experience a life that is governed by emotions, then, by realizing we have the choice to not react emotionally, we master the emotions all together.

Inner peace is vital to living a healthy, happy life, but if we allow our peace to be governed by our emotions and we search externally, then we've already fallen asleep once again and have employed the unconscious state of awareness.

There is much to be said about ourselves as emotional beings and the reality that stems from engaging with the emotions. It's important to be compassionate with ourselves, and handle our fragile emotions. At times, they can seem to rule us, waiting like a ticking time bomb to take over. When this happens, we must remember that we are not our emotions. Our emotions define our experiences but not our hearts. Only love can do that, and love does not need emotions to exist. Love is the constant force inside us all, that safe place we fall back to, regardless of life's situations. Love always has us intimately cradled. We need only to surrender to it.

The beauty of your existence supersedes all material things.

Chapter 5

Ego

To thoroughly understand ego, we must also fully understand its counterpart or opposite, which is love. Now, please don't misunderstand me. The ego is not the enemy, and that is not the idea I intend to create here. Ego provides necessary polarity for growth and evolution, but it must be kept at a minimum. In my experience, with my spirit guides, they've helped me to understand that love is the divine essence of everything that exists. Love does not have boundaries. It is in everything. I believe the words *God* and *love* are the same thing. There is no such thing as existence outside of love, yet love has no boundaries or limits as to where it exists.

Everything in existence has life because, at some level, there is love. Love is the fragrance in flowers, the colors of the sea, the light of the moon, and the gentle breeze through forests. Love is the meaning of peace, and the power in vulnerability. Love is the force that allows faith to carry us through life. Perhaps the most important lesson of love is to know it by experience, and not by knowledge. The two are very different. Allowing ourselves to fully experience love means we become it. We are what we experience, not what we know.

Love cannot be kept within any label, definitions, or boundaries. It is infinite. Love gives life, and anything with life has love at some level. Comprehension of love is not necessary for it to exist. Love is the common thread among all existence and needs no circumstances to prevail. Everything we experience as humans will pass away, except love. Love is immortal. Love is truth.

On the contrary, the ego is indeed mortal, full of fallacies, and conscious of its own mortality. Perhaps the ego's consciousness of its mortality is the byway for all illness. Unlike love, ego needs conditions, events, and circumstances to exist. We often walk the wire between the two.

Ego needs you to exist and to have a place in this universe. It is often in our human nature to give way to the ego and let the ego overrule our actions and even reactions to our own reality. The ego cannot exist without our actions and reactions in it; therefore, when we become the host, the ego becomes the parasite.

You've heard it said before, "The only thing to fear, is fear itself." In life, there truly is nothing to fear. The best we can do is practice complete presence with ourselves, in full, absolute acceptance of all that is.

You see, the ego is housed in fear, and thrives on your guilt. It is rooted in false self-awareness, and experiences an absence of authenticity. The very moment we must employ emotions for a sense of identity, we have fallen victim to the ego. The ego can only exist circumstantially, and though waves of emotions will continually require your reaction for its existence, it is continually fighting death without your response in it. Your ability to express love should not be governed by your emotions; yet, should you deprive the ego, it will only know death because it feeds on your response to your emotions. Your true essence is not based on your emotions.

The ego creates illusions in fear, and in the unconscious state, it is easy to believe the circumstances and conditions that reside in the ego. Transitioning from ego to love and awakening in that process is not an easy process though. In a sense, we experience dying before we become renewed and awakened. Our unauthentic selves dissolve, and our true essence emerges. The harder we fight to maintain an image, or sense of self, the longer we employ ego, for those are all conditions, labels, types, and categories that the ego feeds off of.

I know I've personally been through this struggle, as I battled mentally and emotionally with a modeling career. A fun adventurous career, yes, but in my premature experience, solely based on everything that gives life to the ego. Somewhere, in a deep, intuitive space inside me, this career didn't line up. This journey will be explained a bit later.

In the process of depriving the ego, we renew ourselves in the authentic state of awareness. This is not an easy process though, because it requires us to rid ourselves of conditional thinking, beliefs, and traditions. We must trust ourselves to become aware of ourselves, without any parameters. Sadly, we complicate this process and become addicted to our ego. Because the ego needs our attention and our circumstances to merely exist, it often feels like paranoia or anxiousness as we shed it all together. But I encourage you to have faith in and trust yourself through the process. The divine you, is waiting for you, as you strip away each layer, each mask of the ego, and reveal your true beauty. The essence of you can be found outside every label, and every title you've ever given yourself.

Complexities and difficulties are the normal way of life- to the un-awakened human. It's expected. Accepting the underlying simplicity of our existence as, just of love, can induce confusion. I've seen many individuals yearn for more. They often long for more of an explanation or understanding. But so long as we need to rebuke that simplicity with our questions of understanding, we are still holding on to and giving life to the ego. As long as we're still asking, we've not yet awakened. Accepting is awakening. The ego, though, needs to understand and have control. It does not know faith. Love accepts what is. It is employed through trust and fosters faith.

I'll break it down by explaining what my spirit guides have told me about the truth of ego. As soon as we need to employ emotion to react, we give life to the ego. You see, the ego is not just an inflated sense of self that is totalitarian or boastful. It's not just an awareness that capitalizes on your strengths. It also gives life to our insecurities through doubt and guilt, creating a lack of self-worth and confidence, and it all starts with our thoughts.

Ego is housed in fear, and wherever fear is present, ego will eventually surface, and rear its ugly head. Often, I see people impeach their own self-worth, or even introvert due to their insecurities created by the ego. Not only does ego strive to make up for a lack of knowledge and insecurities through dominance and boast, it will also try to convince you that you're unworthy and not enough. If we react to these thoughts through emotions, we then become enslaved to the ego, but if we can master our minds, we can deprive the ego. Housed in fear, ego provides a disillusioned state of reality and continually leads to struggle.

Ego is also associated with needing, wanting, desiring, and longing, whereas love accepts what is. As we practice the acceptance of what is, without the ego, we seat ourselves in a higher state of conscious awareness. But if we continue to long for something in its absence, we let our heart become our enemy, and the sacred inner space is crowded with ego. We then suffer the consequences and experience a reality of continual deficit.

Ego needs control. It is narcissistic in nature and resists change of any kind, whereas with love, it is the force that perpetuates change. Anything that experiences transformation has life, and anything with life exists because of love. Love is a state of awareness that knows no boundaries and understands that the thoughts of even having control is false awareness. Love accepts what is, and fosters change.

It is very easy to recognize when someone resides in ego or fear, rather than love. These individuals often view the world egocentrically, as if everything pertains to them, for them, and because of them. I have witnessed individuals in this state of mind, experience manic impulsivity and paranoia. Basically, any form of mental illness will reflect a long, intimate history of employing the ego. Sadly though, this often goes misunderstood, unseen and happens subconsciously. The ego creates negative thoughts patterns that exist at a lower vibrational frequency, and once we react to the negative thoughts, mental illness is born. Ego fights hardest when it is raw and bruised through deprivation, but all we must do is let go. You see, when we choose to truly reside in love and deprive the ego, we are freeing ourselves from fear on all levels. Love is everything and nothing at the same time. Think on that for a while. Love cannot be contained within any parameters, yet it is the reason for everything in existence.

When fear becomes the motivating factor behind one's actions, you can bet money that ego will be quick to follow. Sadly,

I often see people become victims of their own ego and develop an addiction to that state of mind. I've seen people cling to and even fall in love with their perception of their reality through ego, only to suffer down the road. As much as I want to help them, I must remind myself it is not my place to change their journey and what they experience. I can only share what has brought me peace.

Every way that you express yourself in your life, and experience your life, is merely a projection of your very own consciousness, so if you believe that you must define yourself through external things, perhaps then, you have not fully connected to the sacred heart. There is nothing wrong with being different and allowing change, but if that individuality is exercised in disregard of mankind as a whole, then we're only hurting ourselves. We are all one, and when we go against the grain of our sacred self in another by treating others poorly in disrespect, we do the same to ourselves.

Free yourself from the burdens of ego, and experience a joyful life of abundance. Part of this requires us to take a deep look at our attachments and detach as much as possible, with external things as part of our identity. This takes bravery and deep self-trust. As soon as we cling to something, we no longer can have it, or enjoy it. We cling through fear of loss and, then develop an attachment. Perhaps this is the phase where we get stuck or confused in compiling our sense of identification. We cling to external things, believing they create our identity. We develop attachments in the false belief that, if we don't have them, our identity will suffer. This is another illusion of the ego. Attachments weigh us down and keep us stuck. As we identify with our attachments, it perpetuates the resistance to change, and creates stagnancy.

In this day and age, ego is everywhere. It lives when we decide to let it in, and host it. It's a choice. When we do, we step into its illusion and experience suffering through it. Ego provides needed polarity against love, in order for us to grow and evolve from situations. But when we choose to reside in ego, this is when we choose a life of suffering over a life of peace.

A great teacher doesn't forcefully impart knowledge to the student; rather, a great teacher opens minds and hearts and fosters the student's ability to become self-directed, self-reliant, and innovative without becoming self-righteous.

Chapter 6

Dying to Live

As a medium and spiritual coach, I deal with death on a daily basis, but not in the way you'd expect. Sure, I bet you're thinking I coach people daily, on how to cope with the loss of a loved one. While this is true, I've actually witnessed more death among the living, than in the dying and discarnate souls. I used to be one of them. A little confusing, I know, but stay with me here.

As humans, we actually experience death, daily, personally, as we host the ego. As I have mentioned, characteristics of the ego create continual suffering on a personal level, in an intimate way. We face death every day, as we host the ego. It has no life without us, our attention to it and reaction, in it. Yet when we surrender it completely, death occurs. Death of the old self-awareness, beliefs, and thought patterns and new life is realized. Many individuals are afraid of death, on many levels, and that is why the ego seems to be so prevalent. We cling to it subconsciously.

This is the very place I have found myself while coaching many individuals. They experience death and dying, as they cling to life, and expectations, instead of surrendering to what is. We cling to the life and reality that it has made for us, and often will do whatever we can, in our power, to maintain a sense of self, that is derived from the ego. Chasing that identity, is continual employment of death. Clinging to our expectations is dying. We deprive ourselves, of knowing our inner divinity, as we turn ourselves inside out for the ego's pleasure. We're not really living, and don't have pure self-awareness, while stuck amid this chase. We step into a losing battle, an illusion, and die as we fight to maintain the illusion.

I have come to understand too that judgement, rooted in ego is another form of death. If we must employ judgment upon ourselves, or against others, we die in that process. We deny ourselves the true reality that abides, and label it instead, through ego. Judgement against others, only reflects the self-rejection within, employing death. Striving to be something else, we die.

We inflict unnecessary pain, discomfort, and harm upon others and ourselves in the process.

Personally, I have been a victim in the past of my own ego, before I woke up and truly understood it all. My downfall was control. I was dying to be in control of situations and outcomes. In the desire to have control, I found myself dying, many times, in a 'power struggle' with others. I'd suffer the losses, or the belief that there even was something to lose. I've come to realize that nothing is in my control, and if I surrender to the divinity of the universe, beautiful things are bound to happen.

As I type this, I can already hear my reader's thoughts, "Well, how do I do that? How do I actually surrender and trust the universe?"

I say this to you, "Uphold inner space in your heart for inspiration, and surrender to something greater than yourself. The simultaneity of these will be the necessary channel for divine will to take place in your life and help you to experience living."

An example I'll share, almost convinced me to hang it up all together, and ignore mediumship. You see, in the work I do, as a medium, it's not uncommon to be asked to remotely view something. I've done this many times personally, but never for anyone else to gain insight. I used to think—or rather believe—that it was invasive. Now I know that, if it's achievable, there's a reason.

Last year, I had one particular client who had sessions with me, almost weekly. Her sessions were for her personal growth, through spiritual coaching. I channeled my guides for her, and we discussed many things.

One day, she decided to change it up a bit and try something very unique in our session. In the beginning of our conversation, she told me that, as we were speaking, her mother was in the operating room in another state, having open-heart surgery. She asked me if my guides could take me to the operating room and show me how the surgery was going, since she couldn't be there physically.

Having complete faith in my guides, I quickly said, "Well sure!"

I had no idea, what I was getting myself into. As I said, I have done remote viewing in the past, but nothing to this degree.

So, I saw my guide reach out for my hand. I took his hand and allowed myself to go with him. In this experience, there was no sense of travel really, just a shift in focus. We suddenly were outside of the operating room, looking in.

I told my client, "I can see your mother on the operating table. She's already under, and a spirit woman, Pam, is in the hallway."

I didn't tell my client that the spirit loved ones I saw, around her mother were crying. I felt like I wasn't supposed to tell her, so I kept that part to myself.

My client replied, "Oh my gosh! That's my Aunt Pam! My mom's sister!"

I continued to absorb as many details as I could, so I panned around the room, and saw a mother and father in spirit, hovering in the right corner of the room. I told my client. They too were crying.

"Yes, both of her parents are deceased."

At this point, I checked in with my guides. As I looked over, my guide looked at me, over his left shoulder. He and I were still holding hands as he said, "Kim, she's cold."

My immediate response was ignorant, but I have to own it! I looked at him and said "Duh! It's an OR, and they are always freezing."

He left me in my belief of this thought, and shifted his focus back to my client's mother, in surgery. It was interesting. Every time my guide shifted his awareness, I automatically experienced his new area of focus, simultaneously with him. It's fascinating to me, still.

At this point, my guide took me above, in an aerial view of the surgery. I could see her bright white ribs, open and pointing upward almost, to the ceiling. I could see the surgeon's hands, with blue gloves on, clamping blood vessels around the heart. The background noise of monitors, and the machines beeping seemed to get louder and louder. Now, as I looked closer, I could see four hands, surgeon's hands, holding her heart. The heart stopped beating. I noticed this, but it didn't alarm me. I had no idea, that the heart actually does stop, during this type of operation.

At this point, my guide looked at me and said, "Kim, there's no pulse."

Again, in my ignorance, I replied, "Well yeah! They just stopped her heart."

Again, my guide said nothing in response and left me to ponder my idea. I was missing his guidance. Next, I looked over, and witnessed gray energy, leaving the patient's body from the center of the chest. I told my client all of this. Now, as a medium, I perceived this as negative energy leaving the body, and that was what I told my client.

Boy, was I wrong. Our session time seemed to quickly come to an end, although her mother was still in the operating room. My guide brought me back into grounded awareness, and the viewing dissolved. This client of mine, so faithful to her growth, recorded every session. This one was no exception.

Later that evening, she sent me a text message to inform me that her mother died on the operating table. She didn't make it through the surgery. Her legally recorded time of death, was the exact last minute, of our recorded phone session before we hung up.

When I got the news, the reality of what I had just witnessed came full circle, and hit me like a swift punch in the gut. I thought I was going to be sick. I didn't know whether I should be grateful for such clarity, or sad and overwhelmed.

The gratitude came later. I had to saturate and process what the hell just happened. I remotely viewed this lady making her transition, during her surgery. My guide was giving me the signs the entire time, but I was too stubborn to pay attention to him.

I should have known by the grim look on his face, each time he spoke to me, "She's cold, Kim. There's no pulse, Kim."

It all made perfect sense now, but gosh darn it, I would have never guessed that I was actually watching this woman pass away, and leave her body! And I thank God, I didn't understand it at the time, because I would not have had the heart, to tell my client. At the time, it was more than I could bear. It made me sick. It was so real, and the duality of it had me sickened for a few days. I canceled my sessions for the rest of the week as this evolutionary experience set in. The responsibility hit me deeply. My client conveyed her understanding, of what I had witnessed and translated to her live, as it was happening. Looking back, and listening to the session again and again, she understood the guidance as it was coming through.

This story and this example certainly made me question if I have what it takes to continue doing this type of work. Trust me, at this point, with this level of truth occurring, I didn't think I could go on, if this kind of stuff were going to continue happening. As I often do, I turned to my guides and asked for their input.

They smiled, with a 'matter-of-fact' tone and said it was only a big deal because I was afraid of death and because I was making it a big deal.

"You witnessed a birth, Kim, not a death. Don't you see? What are you afraid of?" They were leaving it up to me, to figure out.

With this experience, and the help of my guides, I had to accept that I was afraid of death, and that was what gave me such trouble. I had to do some deep self-evaluation to discover the root of my fear. It went back to my need for control and certainty. I realized I was not actually afraid of death, but uncertainty. This too, I have come to realize is rooted in ego. You see, as we let go of the ego, it dies, and I was clinging to false awareness through ego.

This example, and many others have helped me to see what death actually is. It has nothing to do with the physical form really; it has everything to do with the ego, and the fallacies associated with it. We suffocate our lives and our ability to be free, by chasing what we don't have. We die a little every time we long for something because we are desiring through the fear of loss. We subconsciously acknowledge the absence and perpetuate it. When one begins to long for something, he or she becomes trapped in the experience of its absence. Longing exists in the acknowledgement of absence, creating suffering and emotional death. Not physical death, but death of the heart, pure consciousness, and true living.

Allow yourself to die so you can live.

Chapter 7

Awakening

Love is life, and anything with life is love. This is the common thread among us all, and as we awaken to it, we also awaken ourselves to our highest potential. It's the universal thread that connects us all. Only when we give life to the ego do we separate ourselves from this common thread.

When we allow our happiness to be influenced by earthly (material) things, that happiness will continually escape us. Material possessions don't last, and neither will the happiness we subject to them. We will quickly become a victim of our own ego. When our awareness and actions are experienced through ego, happiness, joy, fulfillment, and so on, they will be dependent upon conditions and circumstances, essentially giving life to the ego. It begins to perpetuate itself, like a biofeedback system. It is only when our happiness can supersede all material things, much like the Buddha taught us, that we truly awaken. Then, true, absolute happiness is not conditional at all. It is pure. This is consciousness.

Awakening to our own personal enlightenment, though, seems like a difficult task to achieve, let alone maintain. A series of evolutionary experiences usually becomes the catalyst behind one's awakening process. How many times throughout life have we seen individuals make a drastic change, through circumstances, and evolve or awaken? These experiences can include, a traumatic event, loss of a loved one, divorce, or job loss and can even occur among the process of self-exploration. As we progress through these phases, and experience our own polarities, hopefully the result becomes complete self-awareness at the most authentic level. As we become aware of our being, through these phases, and realize that the phases actually have nothing to do with us at all, that they are just experiences, we begin the awakening process.

These phases may affect our state of being but do not make up our being. When our ability to understand self, and is maintain self-awareness, without it being affected by the outside world, we begin to awaken and align with our higher level of consciousness. As we align with the pure self, that resides in our sacred inner space, we naturally acquire consciousness within our purity, and realize that our peace cannot be disrupted. That disruption is only an illusion, created by our thoughts, that we give way to. We chose that interaction with our thoughts and emotions. We put it on, like a coat and wear it. The beautiful thing is the moment we realize we don't have to engage. We don't have to wear the coat. It's just a mask.

It's pretty simple. We have the choice to react, and how we'll react. But, even knowing that we have that choice, also requires higher levels of consciousness. Just as easily, we can turn the other cheek. Understanding that we don't have to give way to anything and react, we naturally nourish the peace within the inner space of ourselves. Nothing can affect us, and make us unhappy, or disrupt our peace unless we react and allow it to.

This reminds me of the teachings I have learned through my personal relationship with Yeshua (I use Jesus and Yeshua interchangeably). He has often taught me that, when one resides in ego, and ego being false awareness, one cannot take accountability for one's actions. The ego cannot host accountability because the ego itself does not exist, it is not truth. It is an illusion, that creates false realities. Therefore, individuals in ego will project their emotions, thoughts, and feelings on others. Then, when we react, we engage the lower basic self. As we do this, we open ourselves and host what the egoic individual is projecting. It becomes like a parasite and can damage our hearts if we aren't mindful.

Yet, through heart-centered awareness, we can remain neutral to what others are projecting. We can choose not to host the parasitic emotions that ultimately lead to guilt, and suffering. When someone is unhappy with themselves at some level, they will project that through the ego. It is in our highest good, to be aware and not engage. When we engage, we become.

You see, it'll only affect you, if you accept it. Transmute the negativity so you don't transmit it. As we grow within our inner space and reside in that peace, the simplicity that it is, is like a huge epiphany. As you connect to your inner place of peace, a newfound trust in the universe is strengthened. A whole new world begins to unfold within you, as you reconnect with your personal power, within. Fears, doubts, and worry that once filled your heart will fall away, and your sacred inner space will abide. You naturally become a being of a higher vibrational frequency, residing in love. Here, nothing can touch you and, affect the essence of you now, in this space.

This state of awareness is nirvana, which fills your soul as you awaken to the realization that your being will always supersede its environment. Your situation may change, in thousands of ways, but you're still you, through it. Your being is the constant, unwavering existence amid the chapters of the universe. The realization that your existence is a projection of your awareness, your thoughts, and the way you engage with your thoughts determines your life experiences. Scenarios come and go, time will pass by, and events and circumstances will dissolve, yet, the essence of you, your being, will remain. Your consciousness and awakened state to it will prevail.

This is freedom on an entirely new level, when you truly embody the understanding of your life purpose and its boundless nature. Achieving this state of super consciousness must come from within, and your willingness to let go of all attachments, and lay down all barriers. It is a complete state of surrender that nurtures inner peace.

I've often come across many individuals who have lost their sense of purpose. If we seek purpose in external things and doings, we may continually feel purposeless. We must look inward, and realize that our very being, *is* our purpose. That fact that we are living, being creatures, is our purpose. We then exercise free will to expand our consciousness, and awaken.

If we introvert our efforts in building ourselves, as much as we extrovert our efforts in building our image, our personal evolution might pleasantly surprise us. Exince with fulfillment beyond all conditions unfolds, and true enlightenment is realized.

As I grow and evolve as a medium and spiritual coach, I have quickly learned that, the more I practice acceptance, the more I nourish my own soul. That nourishment exists in a place that is not contingent upon expectations and outcomes. It is the sacred inner space of my heart. The more we all practice acceptance, the more we'll bring ourselves into a divine state of consciousness. As long as we argue with reality, we will become a victim of our own ego and often become enslaved to it.

Hopefully at this point, you've realized that, whatever we resist, we become. If we resist something—anything—we have not yet realized our attachment to it. Resistance gives life to it in our reality. Whether we are resisting situations, circumstances, or even people, the resistance is the force that perpetuates our misery. Once we allow ourselves to surrender all together, we strengthen the foundation of our inner place of peace, our true home. Most of the time, we resist something through fear.

I've personally experienced being victim of my own fear and resistance. You see, as a mother, I used to have a crippling fear of my children becoming ill, and I would resist it with everything in my power, only to later realize that, through fear, I manifested the situation I was trying to resist. It seemed my kids used to get sick all the time, and as I evolved in consciousness, I surrendered to my fear and stopped resisting. Their illnesses now seem to be few and far between. As soon as I surrendered, my fears and anxieties melted away, as well. I simply realized I had the fears, but I didn't have to host them. I surrendered the need to control their health, and in doing so we've all come out ahead.

Personally, I think achieving an enlightened state is simple. The maintenance, though, is where hard work and effort are required. But anything that requires hard work, will usually always bring you to a more evolved version of yourself. In this secular world, we must continually observe ourselves to maintain mindfulness, another key component of sustaining inner peace. As we practice self-observation, our actions and the way we engage with others will become clearer. We'll maintain a constant state of peace as the world around us unravels.

Practicing mindfulness, though, is key to maintaining the enlightened state. It is a matter of observing our actions and ourselves from a higher perspective, without engaging or reacting, or without thinking or analyzing. Sadly though, absentmindedness prevails in the fast world we live in. I can't even begin to tell you how many times I've said or heard someone say, "Remind me to get trash bags at the store." In asking someone to remind us, we're telling the universe that we'll forget. We're already putting it out there. It takes practice. Mindfulness of our thoughts and mindful engagement with our thoughts makes all the difference.

It is no secret that our thoughts and emotional reactions to them create the reality that we experience. Only when we react to the negative emotions and engage with them do we experience anxieties. When we believe in our fears, anxiety is born. We can disarm our anxieties by cultivating loving, compassionate relationships with everyone, and everything around us.

This world can ask so much of us. We must challenge ourselves to grow, but not ask something of ourselves that simply isn't practical. Sometimes, as you experience your own spiritual awakening, you'll begin to see death and new life. Death of old relationships, prior lifestyle patterns, previous habits, and the things that once were important to you seem to become irrelevant. New interests will take over, and new behavioral patterns will take place in your life. Personally, the trigger that started the ripple effect in my spiritual growth was—and still is—saying yes to myself. The more I say yes to myself, in self-approval and self-forgiveness (saying yes to self-love), the more I've witnessed my own actions in self-love, nurturing my spiritual growth. I've broken down the barriers between myself, and me. I stopped arguing with my reality and myself. I've revealed the mind-centered me and the heart-centered me. The mind-centered me clings to the ego. The heart-centered me, the sacred inner place, has never met the ego. They cannot simultaneously exist in the same place because the heart is love and the ego is fear. So, say yes to yourself, and experience the miracles that await.

As I began this simple mantra, I shredded through these layers of my old self. I was inspired to write this following piece about the process:

Loving an awakened woman. What do I mean by 'awakened?' Well, to me, this is a woman who knows her worth, completely. A woman who has awakened to her truth in God. A woman who knows her value is not bound to earthly material things. When a woman has truly awakened to her truth in God, she becomes fearless in all aspects of life. She sees opportunity where others perceive obstacles. Loving an awakened woman is not an easy task, for she knows and accepts no boundaries. A woman awakened to her truth realizes that her personal power is beyond man's ability to control and can only be empowered, not tamed. A woman who has awakened to her truth knows her value and easily recognizes when something asks her to be less. She is turned on with great desire to empower others, so they too can know their worth. An awakened woman knows her creative nature and often utilizes it to uplift others. A woman truly awakened is unstoppable in her pursuit of happiness, joy, and her ability to transfuse that into others' lives as well. Loving an awakened woman is not easy because she is not like most, continually seeking change to foster expansion and growth. An awakened woman finds no purpose in comparison, but often others feel threatened by her because they compare. Others who have not yet awakened to their divine infinite truth will always criticize and compare because of the ignorance to their own personal divinity.

The woman awakened to her divinity knows that judgment and comparison are illusions that feed the ego, and she knows ego has no place in her heart. The awakened woman exudes self-love beyond the common man's understanding, and is often criticized of being egocentric or totalitarianistic, in her views. The awakened woman's heart cannot be tamed, for it sees God in everything and is passionate about all things, running fearlessly through life while chasing her dreams. An awakened woman has continual space for growth and evolution within herself and the freedom to share that with others without limits. An awakened woman will often do and say things one may never understand, but attempting to control her through your fears will only leave you standing in your own burning house. Loving an awakened woman requires strength, courage to be yourself, confidence in your own understanding of God's affinity for you, and understanding of your own personal truth so you are not threatened by the expression of hers. Knowing your divine truth in God, is perhaps, the only way, or the best way to love an awakened woman. Change is inevitable. We all know this. But the more we accept the change and allow the newness into our hearts, the better life experience we'll have.

Unfortunately, all too often, our hearts and minds are crowded with expectations, and attachments. When we keep our hearts crowded with these things, we leave little to no room for growth and achieving the awakened state.

Life doesn't always go as planned, but that's the beauty of it, for that is when we have the perfect opportunity to grow. Life is continuously providing opportunities for growth, and as long as we trust ourselves to take a leap of faith, we'll grow in the process. Faith, though, is the key. We must trust ourselves enough, to get to know ourselves through our faith.

Some things you must believe, to see, sobelieve in yourself, and see a new you! Our ability to manifest what we want in our lives with the help of the universe, is perhaps, because we essentially, are the universe. We are not energetically separate from it; rather it's a common thread among the totality of the universal flow of life energy. In other words, the common thread that holds us all is the life force energy, God. When you come to that knowingness and align with the understanding, knowing you are deeply intertwined with all that is, then understanding your ability to manifest and create the life you want for yourself becomes like second nature, and even automatic. A deeper self-trust is born. Your existence resides within the universal flow of life force energy; therefore, it is the universe. It is you, and you are it. Perhaps you see synchronicities in life happen all around you. It's not because you are awakening to something, but rather you are aligning with your true essence, the rhythm of life. That rhythm is in everything, and once you align with it, you synchronize yourself with it instead of resist it. The reality you experience is a mere reflection of your consciousness.

Therefore, I always encourage people to be mindful about what they do with their thoughts because the universe and your subconscious can translate them very literally. And as in earlier examples, you could wind up manifesting something you don't really want.

Similarly, as we sail through life, we all have been guilty of putting our most precious aspirations and goals at the mercy of 'someday.' For example, "Oh, someday I'll start my own business" or "Someday I'll make that change." But I tell you, if you toss your valuables into the "someday" abyss, they'll never happen. Someday will never come, and you'll never manifest what you want if you define it by "someday."

You see, someday has no definition. It is false awareness. It doesn't exist. "Someday" does not have the ability to manifest anything for you, because it, itself, does not exist. So, when you put your dreams and aspirations into the "someday" black hole, they too, will cease to exist. The idea of manifestation is to be definitive and descriptive, but not to a point that you develop an attachment and limit yourself or the manifestation. If you want to manifest something, speak it as if it exists in the present moment and aligned with the emotional reality of it.

I encourage you to take a second look at everything you have packed up into "someday" and begin to dig out those treasures, and be more descriptive and definitive to them so you can manifest that which is most important to you.

So, remember to always keep your thoughts in a place of love and light. Align with the universe within, and experience your universe on the outside. Awakening is an amazing process of pure self-realization. As you shed layers of your old self created in ego, you and others will notice your behavior change. You'll find yourself with less need to react to situations, and a deeper capacity to accept all that is. Others will express to you, how you've changed. Understand that they may be speaking from a place that is attached to the old you, resisting acceptance of the awakened you. Love them for where they are in their consciousness. I have gone through this firsthand with almost everyone I know.

As mentioned in other chapters, I've even been ridiculed for who I am. But nothing feels more real than just saying yes to myself. Many of my friends and family have expressed the changes they've seen within me, and at times, they sit back with wide eyes. I'm comfortable with it though, and you should be too, as awakened consciousness is achieved. Standing in your truth is the most powerful thing you can do.

Every once in a while, you must let yourself get swept up in the current

of the universe. Loosen your grip, and let the world inspire you. Try

new things, see new faces, breathe the air of new places, grow in

adoration of diversity, laugh amid the noise of your life, live beyond

your fears, dance to the beat of someone else's drum, throw yourself

into the chaos of change, and be brave in the face of fear. This is

your life to color wildly. Don't use the same colors over and over.

Chapter 8

Harmonious Mind, Body, and Soul

Harmonious relationships among mind, body, and soul are essential for us to live the best lives possible, as we grow in our awakened selves. The deep level of intimacy among the three, at the energetic level, cannot be severed. Each of these is like a biofeedback system to the other, continually receiving and dispensing information from one part to another. We cannot ignore that one part of this system, affects the others, no matter which one it is. If issues arise spiritually, it won't be long before it manifests physically and affects us mentally, as well.

Everything is energy and begins at that level. Anything that has form, solid matter, is still energy. This simple fact has been proven time and time again by brilliant scientists through the years. Knowing this, we must nurture our energy bodies, our spiritual selves, and that will foster good health in our physical selves. Mindfulness about this connection, is key. Understanding the way they directly affect each other can bring us to a deeper level of self-awareness. As we develop this deeper level of self-awareness, we can become so in tune with ourselves, that, when something within us is not harmonious with the rest of us, it is easy to find and change. We cannot engage with the mind and expect it to be an individual interaction, separate from the body and soul. Each one affects the others. We simply just need to practice mindfulness of the intimate connection among the three elements of ourselves—mind, body, and spirit—and equally love each part.

Nowadays, spiritualism is a hot topic and is becoming a fashionable mask for the ego, if we aren't careful. Yogis are popping up everywhere, and it seems meditation is talked about more now than ever. Don't get me wrong. This is a good thing. I personally love yoga and practice many forms of meditation. But I also think there is much more under the surface, that most haven't become aware of yet.

I've seen many spiritual practices utilized for one to connect deeply to his or her spiritual self: guided meditations, automatic writing, hypnotism, visualization, singing bowls, yoga, Tia Qi,

Reiki, the use of crystals, and so much more. While all of these are great avenues to strengthen our spiritual selves, we must also remember to give the same attention to the health of the physical body and our mental health. If we give all of our attention to developing our *spiritual* health and neglect the *physical* and *mental* health, difficulties will eventually arise with those that we've neglected.

I know for myself that, I spend a lot of time and energy developing my spiritual self. I listen to spiritual and metaphysical audio books. I meditate and occasionally write in my journal, about newfound self-discoveries. Although these practices foster my spiritual growth, one thing I soon realized, was that I'd been neglecting my physical and mental health. I've never been a person who enjoys working out, so forcing myself to do so was, well, just annoying. I enjoy physical activities like hiking, swimming, and running, but plain old exercise didn't interest me.

Similarly, I didn't even think about my mental state. As I buried myself in many different books, in an effort to expand my understanding of my spiritual self and the universe, I didn't even notice that I was causing my own mental fatigue. I already have ongoing issues with mental clarity and fatigue, from the head injury I sustained in my car accident back in 2015. Mental stress seems to call the symptoms right back, and it did when I didn't give myself breaks and nurture my mental health. Bouts of severe dizziness and vertigo would come marching back in. Forgetfulness, extreme hypersensitivity to sound, confusion, hyper agitation, and disorientation would happen all over again, like it was just after my accident.

As these symptoms came back, time and time again, it didn't take long for me to realize what was happening. I'd spent too much time nurturing my spiritual growth and health, that I'd neglected my mental health, which it affected my physical health.

This experience was like a battle. At times, it kept me from doing the things I love. When the vertigo was so bad, all I wanted to do was sleep, so I didn't have to experience the dizziness and nausea. I had been going through vestibular and cognitive rehabilitation from the lingering effects from my accident, and I was given a home exercise program to continue my own.

Earlier this year, my mom and I flew to my sister's home to stay and visit for a week. My sister Tiffany, is in the army and stationed in Oahu, Hawaii, and of course I was going to take full advantage of visiting her there. We had so many wonderful adventures planned. If you haven't been to Hawaii, let me tell you, it is worth your time and money to go, at least once. The beauty will bring you to your knees in awe, and demand a hush over your soul as you admire your surroundings. It truly is like another world there, and I was determined to see as much of it as possible.

One of the adventures we had planned was a surprise Mother's Day gift for our mom. She absolutely adores sea turtles, and she loves paddle boarding. So, we booked a stand-up paddleboard (SUP) -sea turtle tour. We'd rent the boards, paddle our way to a turtle cove, drop anchor, and swim with the turtles. It was bound to be a fantastic experience!

We had two gentlemen with us who were our guides for the tour. It was going to be great, our own private SUP sea turtle excursion in Hawaii. Well, they had a blast. I, on the other hand, was making deals with the man upstairs, as long as he'd keep me from getting sick in front of everyone. I wasn't sea-sick. I was practically raised on a boat, so I know I don't get sea-sick. But my vertigo was probably the worst it's ever been, and not wanting to complain, and hold the group back, I paddled my way out to sea. We paddled for at least thirty to forty-five minutes.

The ocean was actually pretty calm for the most part, once we got away from shore, but it didn't matter. I felt horrid. I was so dizzy that, I couldn't even stand up to paddle. I had to sit on my knees. We dropped anchor, and the group swam and snorkeled with the sea life as I floated and clung to my board, struggling with my snorkel gear. Boats began to cruise by as they were snorkeling, creating wake. The waves certainly amplified the dizziness and disorientation, and this only increased my anxieties. I didn't want to ruin it for my mom, so I tried not to say much.

We finally began to make our way back to shore. My knees were raw and bloody from sitting on them the entire time, but I only had about fifty feet left, until I got back to shore. I paddled my heart out, and I could not wait to get off the board. As I got close, of course you better believe that I was taken out by a huge wave, and literally slammed up onto the shore. One of the tour guides even commented on my brutal finish. With body and swimsuit intact, I fetched my board and was never so glad to be done with an adventure like that. I'd do it again, and in fact, I have, but I made sure that mind, body, and spirit were all in check before attempting it again.

Looking back, I can laugh at the entire thing now, but I wasn't amused then. I know now, that I should have listened to my body. But I didn't. I pushed through and went along as if nothing were wrong. My vertigo, dizziness, and hypersensitivity to sound were so severe afterwards that it was sickening. I held it together, and when we got back to my sister's, I took the time to complete my vestibular and cognitive rehabilitative exercises. It certainly helped.

Since then, I have taken the time to acknowledge my mental health, and nourish it as well. After all, it didn't serve me at all to nourish my spiritual health when my mental health was so out of balance. I couldn't think straight, and memory loss was embarrassing at times. But I convinced myself that it'd just go away, instead of taking the time to nourish it.

My own experiences, like this one, lead me to the simple realization that, if you don't have health and well-being of one of these three elements, (mind, body, and spirit), you don't have complete health of the rest. When I'm overwhelmed or mentally stressed, taking time for outdoor activities is usually my fix. Whether it's hiking, gardening, swimming, or simply going for a walk, the outdoors is always my fix.

In the past eight years, as I've grown into the awareness of my spiritual self, I've employed many different techniques to strengthen myself spiritually as a clairvoyant medium. One thing I've realized that has stayed with me, is that mind, body, and spirit all need to be on the same page and in harmony with one another, to live the best life possible.

I can recall another example, when all three weren't on the same page and I was suffering because of it. One morning in early spring of 2016, I was helping my daughter get ready for school, just like any other morning. I'd had my morning cup of coffee, and I was gathering my daughter's clothes to help her get dressed. As I bent forward, I felt something in my lower back pop, and I fell to my knees. Instantly the pain was excruciating, and I couldn't walk or move. It took a few seconds for me to even catch my breath. I'd never had any previous back problems, so this caught me off guard and scared the life out of me.

Having a professional background in physical therapy, I knew something was really wrong. I felt like my lower back and pelvic area could no longer support the weight of my body. I was in tears with pain and had to eventually call my mom for help. She came to my home, helped my daughter off to school, and took me into the emergency room.

I'll never forget that walk to the car. It took two people to help me get up and walk, my mom and my sister-in-law. Bearing weight through my lower extremities was incredibly painful, and advancing one leg in front of the other seemed impossible because of the pain. Absolutely nothing I did alleviated the pain.

After my visit to the ER, and a few shots of pain meds later, I was back home. The doctors had no answers for me, and the meds only made me worse. None of this made sense to me. I had no prior history of back problems. I spent the rest of the day over the toilet, trying not to die from the incredibly strong meds they gave me, that made me so sick. It was hell. As I laid on the bathroom floor, I dozed in and out of awareness. I remember thinking to myself, "*Okay, what did I do to manifest this? What am I doing that has manifested this?*"

At this point in my life, I could easily shift my awareness to different areas of my body, and, with the help of my guides, figure out what was going on. As I asked my body what I was doing physically, mentally, and spiritually to manifest this, I was surprised when the answer came so clearly.

You see, the lower back is energetically associated with the root chakra. In short, the root chakra represents the relationships we have in our lives, friendly and romantic, among many other things. As I asked my body what manifested this, I clearly heard that a harmful friendship I was clinging to, was causing my pain and suffering emotionally, and now physically. I'll admit, it's been the most confusing friendship I've ever had, but still I hung on to it. My energy body had already recognized the damage this relationship was doing to me, and it was just a matter of time before it manifested physically. And because the energetic ties of the root chakra reside near the lower back, at the base of the spine, it's no wonder my back went out like it did. As soon as I became aware of this and thanked my higher self for sharing this information, the pain left.

Right then and there, I surrendered to the situation and faced what I'd been denying myself. I had to let go of this friendship. As I was honest with myself, I felt the negative energy of the situation leave my body and exit out my right hip. I was—and still am—dumbfounded really at this entire experience. I consciously asked my body the reason for the physical pain and ailment. It responded with the spiritual and emotional causes, and once I acknowledged that, it was released.

To me, this too was another way that my mind, body, and spirit were demonstrating their connectedness. My mind was aware of what my body was going through, asserted it, and connected to the spiritual body, and as the circuit was completed, the answers surfaced.

I've come to understand that all three—mind, body, and spirit—must be equally nourished, and they will be in sync with each other. If one is off-key, the others usually are too. We must take responsibility to equally develop and foster the health of each one.

Only recently I've started doing yoga. As I do, I have found that this is becoming an active form of meditation for me. It nourishes my physical health, gives my mind a break, and, in turn, raises my vibration and connection to my spiritual self. I also have occasionally practiced Tia Qi, and feel the same way about it, although I'm much more consistent with yoga. I love it. I'm not incredibly flexible like some yogis who have been practicing for years, but I for sure, like the way it makes me feel. It's that simple. When I do yoga, I feel a complete connection between my mind, body, and spirit. My mind, focused on and connected to my body movements during yoga, relaxes me and allows the inner stillness and peace to grow within me. The more I practice my meditations and yoga, the more I appreciate them both. Spending time in each fosters the internal state of nirvana, that sacred inner space. To me, maintaining that inner peace is priceless. As our mind, body, and soul connections strengthen, we'll naturally awaken a feeling of personal empowerment, secure within ourselves, fulfilled and internally blissful.

The following is a meditation for you to strengthen the mind, body, and spirit connection within yourself. Take time to read over it first. Then find a comfortable place and practice it.

Mind, Body, and Spirit Meditation

Before you begin, prepare a few questions that you will ask yourself in the meditation. Take a few moments to settle into a comfortable position. Secure yourself in a place that you will not be disrupted, and close your eyes.

Take in a few deep breaths, each one connecting you further to your body. Observe how you are feeling at this very moment. Observe the mind, the body, and the spirit. Feel your body soften as you deepen your state of relaxation.

Bring your awareness to your toes, your feet, and ankles. Observe what you feel here. Feel them soften and relax as you release all the tension in your feet. Let your feet fall apart as you relax further, and bring your awareness to your knees and hips. Observe what you feel here. Feel your knees soften and relax. Let your hips become loose and soft, and bring your awareness to them. Don't think about anything else, and as thoughts drift in, let them drift by. You do not have to engage with your thoughts at this time.

Feeling the connection between the mind and the body, bring the awareness up through your belly and into the chest. Observe what you feel here. Feel the belly soften and the chest loosen, and relax your body by shifting your awareness.

Next, move to the shoulders and neck. Take a moment to observe what you feel here. Feel the shoulders, elbows, and arms relax and soften. Feel the neck release tension, and deepen your state of relaxation.

Last, bring your awareness to your face and your scalp. Observe what you feel here. Allow the facial muscles to completely relax, and release the tension in your scalp. Take a moment to observe how you feel. Having taken your awareness through the body from the feet to the crown, feel the body completely soft and relaxed.

Now that you are deeply relaxed, leaving worry far behind, shift your awareness to your heart. Once again, observe as much as you can here. Don't force the experience of anything. What do you hear? What do you feel? What do you see? This is your inner sacred space, your place of peace. This is the place where the highest good of all concerned resides. This is the place where God's essence exists within you. Allow yourself to become enveloped by the feeling of love and comfort. Feel it nourish your body as it eases your mind and melts your anxieties.

Knowing that God helps those who help themselves connect to this Godly essence within you and knowing that as you do, you are helping yourself through God's presence in you. Dwell here. Allow yourself to receive any messages that may be spoken to you here. Trust yourself to receive the messages of guidance needed at this time. And if you have questions, ask your heart. Do not force an answer. Simply ask the question, and gently let it leave your conscience. Trust yourself to receive the guidance you seek in the divine timing of the universe.

Spend as much time as you need to in this state of nirvana. Familiarize yourself with the way your body feels when your conscious awareness is here. Is it perfectly relaxed? Notice that your mind is calm and intrusive thoughts have no power here. Imagine yourself becoming transparent, dissolving into your surroundings, and coexisting in complete harmony with everything around you. Awaken to your divine being within.

When you feel you are ready, gently bring your awareness back to your body. Wiggle your fingers and your toes, take a deep breath, and reacquaint yourself with your environment as you come back into awareness. Drink plenty of water, and slowly acclimate yourself back into your normal daily routine.

Feeling recharged, take the time to jot down a few notes about what you experienced.

_____

_____

_____

_____

_____

_____

_____

_____

_____

_____

_____

_____

_____

_____

_____

_____

_____

The deep level of intimacy between mind, body, and spirit cannot be broken. Foster the health of each to live a life in harmony.

Chapter 9

The Art of Surrender

Trust that the universe has you right where it wants you for your best interest at heart. Trust that there is good awaiting you on the other side of your fears and, through self-trust, you'll surrender your fears. The moment we contest that, we lose everything. We fall asleep, back into the unconscious state of mind.

The universe we live in is compiled of rhythmic beats and vibrational frequencies. From one moment to the next, each beat is connected and creates the natural flow of life. Nothing is ever worth disrupting the natural flow of life and interrupting that peace, the universal music that is life. But as soon as we give away our personal power, through resisting what is, we ultimately contribute to our own misery. Far too many times I've seen this happen, and I too used to disrupt my own music.

Only when I learned the art of surrender did I experience true bliss and a deeper capacity to accept what. Probably one of the most memorable moments in me realizing the universe was begging me to surrender was shortly after my car accident. In November 2015, I had recently totaled my car, sustained a severe concussion, and lost my job as mentioned earlier. Shortly after, I knew this was the universe's way of responding to me, but I hadn't surrendered yet. Just a couple weeks later, I was invited to join a very small group of friends for a Reiki share session that would soon become a huge stepping-stone for my personal growth. Reiki share is basically when a few Reiki practitioners meet up and perform Reiki on each other and share the findings.

My friend Ethan was there, and this was only the second time I'd met him. Every time I saw him or looked at him, as a clairaudient, I heard, "If you build it, they will come." I knew this was my guides sharing their best with me, encouraging me to start a metaphysical business, but I didn't know what this meant in connection to Ethan. I barely knew this guy.

I decided to share it with him anyway. I surrendered. To my surprise, he was also thinking about the same thing, to start a metaphysical business. The connection felt magical, like I'd known him forever, and in that moment, I surrendered to the universe.

Later that night, I decided to get on Facebook, and the first thing that popped up on my feed was the phrase, "If you build it, they will come." I laughed aloud and thanked the universe in my state of surrender.

The next day, Ethan shared with me that he'd been reading a book, and to make a long story short, the book provided a system of questions for one to answer and, at the end, gave a set of numbers. One is to look up the numbers in the back of the book, which would provide one's soul's purpose.

When he did, the phrase, "If you build it, they will come," was the one that matched his numbers. Synchronicity at its finest! By January, we'd signed for a business loan and became business partners. We had decided to open this metaphysical shop together.

In this process of preparing to open a shop, one major piece was missing, the location. We didn't have a space to rent, but we'd already set the energy in motion to create it. While on the hunt for a place, I found myself yet again being asked to surrender, this time from my spirit guides. I wanted the shop to be in a town called Zanesville, but my guides kept telling me to consider New

Concord, Ohio. This was my hometown, where I attended high school.

Believe it or not, I actually argued with my guides and told them no way would I consider it. This tiny village was filled with people who would ridicule and probably even shun my idea. I was holding onto my fear. My guides were steadfast and unwavering in their loving support as they reaffirmed their guidance. So yet again, I found myself with a choice to make. Do I cling or surrender? I still remember the moment I decided to surrender and follow their guidance. I turned my car around and headed to New Concord. I found my shop location that same night and signed the lease for it within a week. The more I realized the power of surrender, the more liberated I became through it.

The moment we decide to surrender and simply align with what is, our entire paradigm shifts. An entirely new level of freedom is experienced—freedom from our attachments, negative thoughts, and even negative people. We surrender the need to fix, to cope, to understand, and to resist and to simply accept what is. This is living in pure harmony with the universe.

The art of surrender though can be difficult. And our attachments to control can be suffocating. The attachments reside in the unconscious state of awareness. If we are unconscious in our existence, we'll see the manifestations of displeasing life patterns repeatedly, as our reality reflects our state of awareness.

If there is one thing that the universe will promise you, it's that change is constant and inevitable. Your resistance to that change becomes the byway for misery. Surrender instead. A kaleidoscope of emotions then pulls us through continual rebirth, like a game of tug-of-war.

Surrender, dance to the rhythm of the universe, and experience the abundance it has for you. When the winds of change are blowing, dance with the wind. Go where the wind suggests, and enjoy the dance. The universe is fostering your growth and restoration. Live it, breathe it in, and accept it. Let the need for understanding gently fall away with the past.

The art of surrender is the key to your happiness and unconditional bliss in life. It will require deep emotional honesty though on your part to understand what your attachment is and to surrender the attachment all together. That process of surrender can bring us to a new awareness that creates a new sense of self, the true and authentic self, yet upholding familiarity in that new sense of self as the disillusioned self falls away.

I know many people who would resist change, stating that it causes pain. I think the only time change is painful is when we resist change or cling to the past or to something or someone. Living in a state of truth requires a certain capacity to accept change, accept what is, and become adaptable. Again, it's like a game of tug-of-war. The universe is beckoning with us to evolve and grow, but we pull back as we try to dissolve our attachments to the ego. When you surrender to the current state of reality, you win every time. You envelope yourself in your highest truth, a state of constant surrender, acceptance, and love. This is your truth.

Truth recognizes itself in another. Whether that other is a person, place, or thing, truth knows itself. And as you evolve into true authentic self-awareness, you may be required to stand alone in your truth. Most people are not willing to stand alone. Personally, I'd much rather stand alone in my truth than among a crowd in blind faith.

Most often, the attachment to expectations causes all the pain and resistance. And we are always searching for the next thing to cover up the current thing that we are uncomfortable with, ultimately creating layers upon layers of illusions that separate us from our divine, inner sacred self.

One of the most profound prayers that I still hold dear to my heart is the serenity prayer. This prayer teaches us directly the importance of surrender. "God grant me the serenity to accept the things I cannot change, courage to change the things I can, and the wisdom to know the difference."

This part as a prayer metaphorically teaches us to know when to surrender. It goes on, "Living one day at a time, enjoying one moment at a time, accepting hardships as the pathway to peace, taking, as he did, this sinful world, as it is, not as I would have it, trusting that he will make all things right, If I surrender to his will. So that I may be reasonably happy in this life, and supremely happy with him. Forever and ever in the next. Amen."

All too often, in the midst of arguing with reality instead of accepting it, we sacrifice our inner peace, and in turn, we carry that heaviness on our hearts. Thereupon, the heart becomes the enemy. It beats louder and louder every time we rebuke what it's trying to tell us until we surrender and listen. The heart knows where it needs to go. It's the mind that gets in the way. This can be a painful cycle. However, pain is useful when we finally surrender to it and allow ourselves to learn from it. The good news is: circumstances will always pass, and you'll still be you. So take care of yourself through the storm. Trust what you feel each step of the way. Surrender to the guidance of the universe.

It is what it is until it's different, and learning to accept what is through the art of surrender is the key to absolute joy, one that is internal and not reliant on the outside world for its existence. Accepting what is and, in that sense, surrendering to what is is the state of mind that fosters our ability to transmute the very things that make us unhappy. When we surrender to what is without trying to overpower it, we disarm it from having any capability of affecting our happiness.

For example, in my past, I've encountered many individuals eaten alive by their own jealousy, but instead of reacting through, I know I can disarm them by acceptance and compassion and surrendering to their level of consciousness. It does not mean that I join them in that level of consciousness, but I accept it and surrender the need to react.

This was a hard lesson to learn though. As I look back through my childhood and teenage years, I remember, many times I would disarm my friends' jealousy by humiliating myself so they'd feel less threatened. I would make fun of myself and continually expose my insecurities, thinking it would lift them up and make them feel better. How insane!

If someone's power or work is dependent upon others' insecurities, that is certainly an ego-derived sense of worth. The need to dominate and overpower others comes from the same place. It wasn't until later in life that I would realize that combating their own personal insecurities was not my war. And boy, was it liberating to lay down the weapons and stop participating in that battle. I have found complete freedom in surrender.

A vast part of this too is emotions. If the emotions govern our existence, then we are once again flirting with the ego and operating at a very basic level of self. To expand our consciousness, we must go beyond the emotions and the need to react through our current emotion. There is an intimate connection between our actions and our emotions, but if our emotions govern our ability to love, we have defaulted to the ego.

When you surrender to something, you claim your personal, internal power over it, not in a dominant way but in a way that your personal power and self-worth is not subjected to it. Surrendering is the practice of returning home to that sacred inner space that doesn't need to react to anything to feel a sense of validation.

Love is the only energy that is powerful enough to transmute any other thing. In my opinion, I think resistance to anything is the gateway to suffering. The more we can allow, change, and adapt, the easier our lives will be. As humans though, sometimes it's hard because of the attachments we develop throughout life. Then when one of those attachments is suddenly changed or ripped away from us, we lose ourselves in trying to cope.

One of the most common coping mechanisms that I've seen among individuals trying to deal with discomfort is relocating their place of residency. I have witnessed this with some of my friends and family members. It seems that being in a new place, surroundings, and environment demands vulnerability from us. Vulnerability requires us to be open and honest with ourselves to accept change. Strength through vulnerability allows us to strengthen our self-trust. But the common factor through it all is, no matter how many external changes we make, we must take care of our hearts and our sacred inner selves too.

Dealing with loss will create a change in your life, one way or another. The most important thing to remember through these changes is the way you take care of your sacred inner space. Be as present with yourself as you can, practicing mindfulness in the present moment, and you'll help yourself through the phases of change.

Whatever it may be, we often resist that change and cause ourselves to get stuck in our grief, holding on to the way things used to be instead of living in the present. The loss of a loved one, a job, or a relationship or grief in any form can also require us to be emotionally vulnerable in ways we haven't experienced before. Vulnerability allows us to be open to change and accept what is. Sadly though, all too often, we convince ourselves that we are out of control and allow our grief to consume us.

When we take charge to create change, transformation that may require a deep level of vulnerability, we are stimulated in ways that alter our vibration, shifts our focus, and gives us a push in the right direction toward healing.

From relocating our residence to changing daily routines, adaptability is the common thread that contributes to healing. If we can allow ourselves to adapt to the ever-changing circumstances in life, we won't be tied down to the circumstances, for joy ultimately gives birth to newfound freedom in your life. Yet again, we find ourselves among circumstances to surrender the attachment to "what was" and allow "what is." When something is new and unfamiliar, we must find ways to adapt. Most of the time, that means letting go of old attachments and adapting to the present circumstances.

People and circumstances are powerless without your reaction and attention. The more you resist something, the more you become it. The energy you give something through the resistance is the very force of energy that gives it life. Similarly, if you react to someone or something, you give it life too.

You see, we hold on to pain, and it exists within us until we realize that we're the life source for it. If we stop giving it attention and energy, the pain has no way to sustain itself. It feeds off our response to it.

Although life can be difficult at times, we should embrace the difficulty because it has the potential to be our greatest teacher. It's a matter of choice. It can be our greatest teacher, only if we are ready for truth, if we can surrender the ego. The point is not to avoid your pain. Surrender to it. Feel your pain and your emotions. Let the pain from them bleed out and become fuel for your passion, your drive, and your motivation. This is how you heal. You transmute the source of pain by using it for fuel to your next move. You must develop your own capacity to see the silver lining though.

When we avoid pain and are unable to find peace within, we must remember that, by avoiding it, we still are becoming it. The detours we take to avoid our pain continue to define us. If we are acting at all, it defines our consciousness, and if that action is to avoid something or someone, we are still attached to it and defined by it. In these times of pain and suffering, we abandon our inner sacred self. We all have. We must go to the very place where we abandoned our self-love and trust of the inner divine being and transmute that abandonment to love. We can do that simply by looking for ways to grow with it instead of resisting it.

Seeking joy outwardly is useless. Everything external is an illusion, contingent upon and suspended in time and space. The only constant you'll every truly know is you, your divine self. Everything else will passes away.

We spend a lifetime trying to make memories through our expectations. Often in that process, we forget to be present, to live. We spend time making and building ourselves, but we forget to be ourselves and what that authenticity actually feels like.

Before we know it, we look back through the lens of regret and carry the heavy burdens that come along with it. You see, as soon as we long for something, we are acknowledging the lack of it. If we acknowledge the lack of something through that longing, we perpetuate its absence. Because we all know that what we give energy and attention to, we give life to. We manifest our own current state of reality.

Surrender to what is and trust that the universe

has you right where you're needed.

Chapter 10

The Path of Least Resistance

While living among a "me" culture where secularism and individualism is so prevalent, upholding inner nirvana can be difficult. And yet, if we haven't claimed our personal power, we can easily feel translucent to the rest of the world. Finding the balance is like walking a tightrope. Too much tension results in little to no flexibility, no room for growth, and not enough results in unsteady ground, making us feel lofty. We must create our path with care and great attention to detail. As long as our happiness and joy is subjected to our likeness, then our likeness is all we'll ever know. We won't grow beyond that and experience life outside of that likeness. It's like trying to see the world through a mirror. All you'll ever see is your own reflection. And if there's rejection in your reflection, growth seems impossible.

However, if we can move past our own likeness and step into the unknown, this is the place where unity happens. It is a common ground that we've all visited at one point or another. There is unity here amidst the grounds of uncertainty and vulnerability. This unity far surpasses the false adequacies of the ego. This unity is so divine that it exists here always, without conditions and parameters. We're all hoping for this unity, but we're too afraid to trust for it. The moment we allow ourselves to trust ourselves, we are choosing the path of least resistance. As we employ secularism and individualism, we create resistance in our lives. We must be willing to move beyond these ideations, these false realities, in order to contribute to unity.

Many times, in communicating with my guides, they've reminded me, "What you resist, you become." By resisting something, you give life to it within you. You become it. By resisting, you're reacting, engaging, and becoming.

If there is resistance, there is fear. Fears hold us hostage until they are exiled by incantations of acceptance, transmuting them into fuel for passion and ultimate freedom. We are only a prisoner of our own hell, if we choose to remain a prisoner. When we cling to the things that make our lives difficult, we also surrender the path of least resistance. As we stagnate in our fears at times, held hostage by them, we then become hopeless. Hopelessness sets in and can strengthen the resistance we face. When we allow ourselves to move internally, to adjust, and to adapt, then we pull ourselves out.

The key to maintaining the path of least resistance for yourself is adaptability. This is a fact of nature. In a riverbed, the waters flow around the rocks, adapting to the environment instead of fighting their way through the rocks. You see, just like the waters in the river, we've had the key to our freedom all along. The key to our freedom, to the path of least resistance, is an ultimate state of acceptance and adaptability. As we practice accepting all that is and trust the universal flow of life, we align with the path of least resistance and contribute to our personal happiness.

Choosing the path of least resistance to create a happy life involves a higher level of consciousness. It is an inner knowing of the continual existence of peace and happiness, beyond anything and everything in the material world, that inner place of peace we've talked about all along in this book. That sacred inner place in your heart remains untouched by the outside world. This is your path. Reverting to the heart for guidance will always be the path of least resistance. The true heart has no resistance; it is eternal and boundless. Its boundless nature is pure and absolute love-acceptance. There's no resistance. The peace in residing here is quite simple. Because your being is made of pure love, all you must do is accept that state. It is very simple. Just be in it. Just be.

Unfortunately, in a world that is conditioned by complexities, when something is so simple, it's hard for us to understand and accept it. We reject its simplicity and default to our conditional beliefs in complexity. We actually employ a belief in complexity and sacrifice our inner peace in the process. We often make things more difficult than they are, and, in turn, the circumstances get the best of us. I've seen many people make themselves sick by overthinking something. I call it the "big but" excuse. How many times have you heard someone say, "Well, yeah but…" The good news is that we have the choice to change the way we act and react and choose the path of least resistance.

Sometimes we stand tall in ego with the need to be noticed, heard, seen, and validated. Our searches are propelled by the belief that "There must be more to it" or "It can't be that simple." We begin an inner battle of self-destruction by arguing with reality. The battle itself abandons the path of least resistance. Choosing the path of least resistance only becomes difficult when we give life to ego through the need to control.

This reminds me of an example my guides shared with me a long time ago. They said to imagine a field of colorful wildflowers, growing rampantly across the land. Among this expressive array of flowers, there are colors and species of all kinds. Reds, pinks, purples, yellows, orange, and even white flowers are sprinkled throughout. Although these colors could create division, they don't because of the simplicity of the life force in flowers. Each flower blooms without hesitation, blooming in its own beauty amid its own perspective and adding to the collective beauty of the field, creating unity.

You see, the flowers don't hesitate to bloom due to their fear, in comparison to others. They simply exist in their beauty, inside self-love, coexisting with the others. And as they do, they create unity. This field wouldn't be nearly as beautiful if there were only one type of flower or one color. It takes all of them collectively to make the field beautiful. They all bloom in the same language of self-love, and that creates unity.

You've already mastered what it feels like to be broken because of comparison, to be angry, jealous, powerless, and frustrated. It's content there because you have control, and you know it well. Challenge yourself to step outside of that safe zone, embrace the unknown with trust, and allow vulnerability to have a place in your existence. Vulnerability is built on a foundation of trust, and this is something that takes heart. The environment in which you place yourself can shape your experience, but only when you let go of control and allow yourself to be vulnerable do you experience change and personal growth. So knowing that vulnerability is our personal key to growth and evolution, we must evaluate different areas of our lives where we can allow room for vulnerability.

As we move through life, sometimes at a pace that leaves us dizzy, our disposition can be persuaded. Various events, circumstances, and people can have an effect on our disposition, if we aren't mindful. Thus, a sour disposition can consume us. If we can trust ourselves and surrender the need to react, we'll, in turn, foster our ability to maintain a healthy temperament.

Life changes us, day in and day out. People, events, and life experiences are all beautiful accents to what nurtures our soul and effects our disposition in life. Unfortunately in the world we live in, we are among a fast-paced society that often leaves little to the imagination, and little is kept sacred. But the character you work to maintain will shape your experience here in this world. If we choose to react negatively to a situation, it ultimately leaves us feeling depressed because it lowers our vibration and can even result in poor health. Aligning with our higher self-consciousness will improve our ability to maintain a healthy disposition and give new life to our everyday experiences. This will always be the path of least resistance. Remember, we are all here living our own journeys but walking the same divine path back home. Do what you can to create unity.

The more I observe the world around me, the more I see that fear and anxiety create the path of most resistance as the inner peace is disrupted. Amidst this observation, I decided to ask my spirit guides to elaborate on this subject. The following is a small excerpt of a conversation with my guides.

Me: Can you please shed some light on fear and anxiety? I know so many that struggle with both.

Guides: Of course. Fear is aroused when one denies the true self. When one lacks the conscious connection to the divine self, fear abides. The true self is in the present moment. Anything else will be fear-driven. While in the state of fear, the feeling of deficit will prevail. Man then reacts to the feeling of deficit in false awareness, and that reaction perpetuates the cycle. Fear nourishes fear. It perpetuates itself. Love transmutes it. Fear and anxiety perpetuate each other and need each other to exist. If you deprive one, you minimize the other as well. You deprive them simply by not using them to express yourself.

Me: Can you please also explain anxiety further?

Guides: Anxiety is believing in your fears. Anxiety arises when one is departed from true self and engages with the fears. Man decides to engage by reacting, allowing fear to be his motivation, placing himself in the illusion his fear has created, further divorcing from his inner divinity. Do not be the echo of your own fears. Sit within your inner heart, departing from the temptation to give life to your fears. Hush them through love. Love your fears, for they exist at a place that does not know divinity. Treat them with compassion. Love them, and experience their transmutation. If you host them, you become them. If you love them, you transform them. You must first practice acceptance. Accept all that is in your life, your complete awareness and reality. Fear arises when you argue with your own reality, and anxiety follows when you believe your fears. When you deny reality or try to avoid it, you begin having delusional thoughts, behavior, and awareness. Accept what is. Don't overlook the value in your daily life. Acceptance is the key to happiness. Realign your thoughts, feelings, emotions, and awareness to the present moment, and you'll minimize your fears and anxieties.

Me: Okay, so how do we help others suffering in this way?

Guides: Acceptance. Teach them what adaptability is. Remind them. They mustn't believe in their fears that they have created. When one practices adaptability to the circumstances, one will contribute to their own evolution. Show them that they are accepted. That will foster self-acceptance within.

Me: Doesn't all of this come from ego?

Guides: Yes. Ego houses fear and illusions. Fear houses anxiety, both are lower vibrations. Lower vibrations lead to illness. If you are residing in an egocentric vibrational frequency, fear, doubt, depression, and anxiety is all you'll ever know. Illness can easily manifest in these vibrational fields— mental, physical, and spiritual. This is again being disillusioned from true self. Practice the surrender of expectations to experience a true state of awareness. Let go of expectations and burdens. They too are false awareness. Trust in the essence of your personal truth, and the fallacies of your false self will melt away. Always keep room in your soul for God and personal growth, and open your heart to new adventures!

Here are a few easy tips from my guides that will help:

- Don't worry. It kills life in all things associated with it. Trust instead.

- Begin each day with meditation or prayer. You will strengthen your will/motivation.

- Don't envy. It's a waste of time and perfect energy.

- Spend time alone to know yourself without electronics. Trust yourself.

- Accept your limitations. Be easy on yourself. You are human and can only accomplish so much in a day's time.

- Have faith in humanity. Give love through trust. Cynicism sours your disposition too.

- Control your appetite. Eat to live; don't live to eat. Overindulgence clogs the body, mind, and spirit.

- Find a hobby. It will foster inner peace.

- Find ways to increase your selfless acts on a daily basis.

- Do everything in love. If it cannot be done in love, don't do it.

I want to expand on each of these briefly. As an Army wife, a mother, a sister, and especially a medium, these dynamics have offered diverse perspective. I have seen so many people, some even close relatives, who live in fear and worry. For those who are fear-stricken, I've even seen them capitalize on their fear. As stated, fear and worry kill life. Anytime one acknowledges a fear, he or she is depriving themselves of love. As I also said before, love is life, but fear kills both. Acknowledging fear though isn't necessarily the unwanted part. Its actions through fear or rather motivation from fear makes all the difference.

If we shift our perspective by utilizing prayer and meditation instead of motivation by fear, we'll manifest a life of abundance. Strengthen your will and motivation through prayer and meditation, not through fear.

We've all heard many times that comparison is the thief of joy and often gives life to jealousy. If we chose to employ these thoughts and emotions, we are wasting perfectly good energy to poison our own disposition. You are you regardless, so practice accepting that without the need to compare. Utilize the pure divine energy within you to manifest the best life possible.

Next, if we can trust ourselves to be alone with ourselves, true personal power is realized. I've often heard many individuals consider introverts as a bad thing or people who prefer to be alone as unhealthy. Personally, I believe that, if one is comfortable being alone, this demonstrates strong personal power. We need to practice the detachment from electronics and the need to be entertained and trust ourselves to be alone. Be curious about yourself. Be as curious about yourself as you are about the world around you. As we take time for ourselves and personal self-discovery, we gain universal wisdom by knowing ourselves on every level possible.

As we gain new perspectives of our self through spending alone time with our self, we must also acknowledge our human limits. We are all human. We all make mistakes, and we all have limits. Accept them. Work hard, but surrender your expectations. Expectations are illusions that divorce us from our ability to know our true selves. If we spread ourselves too thin and overexhaust ourselves, we'll only contribute to compromised state well-being. Give yourself compassion more often in accepting your limits.

As we grow in our ability to accept our personal limits, this will foster a stronger faith toward humanity. For if we can see and accept our own imperfections, we can also pass that acceptance along to others as well. Even imperfections are an illusion, but I'll try not to stray too far from the subject at hand here. Going back to the concept that we are all one, all trying our best in our current state of consciousness as we accept our personal limits, we hopefully can achieve that toward others as well. As we do, the veils of judgement will be removed, and we'll be able to truly see the beauty in humanity once again. This requires trust. As we employ trust, on some level, we are becoming a channel for love.

Further, as we continue our journey of self-discovery, we must remember the importance of physical health. We must eat to live, not live to eat. If our eating is imbalanced, so is our life. Imbalanced eating leads to unhealthy behavior and vice versa. Both can lead to clogged mind, body, and spirit.

Additionally, time spent in your favorite hobby will foster inner peace. As you envelop yourself in your hobby, you rekindle the connection to your inner self, the place of peace I've been speaking about throughout this book. The stronger connection you maintain to your inner heart space, your place of peace, the more consistently you'll be a being of calm, loving energy.

Be as curious about yourself as you are about the world around you.

Chapter 11

A Life with Purpose

I decided to add this chapter to this book simply because I've encountered so many individuals who still long to learn their purpose here in life. As I connect with my guides, the answer is always the same across the board, no matter who I'm speaking to. This is what they say:

*First, as long as you are looking and searching for your purpose, you have not yet woken up. Like a hamster on a wheel, you'll keep running through life, feeling lost in your own illusions. You'll always experience the absence of purpose and lack of fulfillment. **You must understand that your purpose is not to do, but rather to be.** That is it. But many individuals cannot accept the simplicity in that. They make life harder than* *it is, searching for more and, in turn, birthing their own anxieties. Among a culture conditioned by complexities, simplicity seems wrong and non-trustworthy. This is what happens when one believes in the illusions the mind creates. **Your purpose is not to do, but to be.** The very fact that you have awareness, life, and breath is your purpose. In essence, God is the life within you, and God is experiencing Himself through you.*

The tragedy isn't *not* knowing the essence of your purpose. The only real tragedy in life is when we silence our inner child. There is an inner child inside us all, still willing to believe in the magic of the world. An inner child is leading faith, hope, and love for the world. An inner child is more aware of the present moment than anything else. The inner child in us all is our purest place of trust and vulnerability. In times of hurt and despair, we must trust our inner child and allow healing to occur there. Give new life to the purity of the inner child within you.

We must be devoted to ourselves and passionate about loving our inner child. This is the place where pure hope and faith in the world reside. This is where our sense of purpose is known, where our sense of purpose resides without the need for external validation.

Years before I grew into my mediumship, I began an early career in modeling. As I mentioned earlier, this was a trying time because I found out who my true friends were. In 2004, I packed up my life and road-tripped all the way from Ohio to Miami with my mom. Everything in the world seemed perfect, like a careless breeze passing through my hair. With a contract with Wilhelmina Modeling Agency on the table, I was planning to relocate and move to Miami. I was so excited, and I couldn't wait to get there! My modeling career was about to take off. I had many smaller modeling jobs locally and was ready for my big break, or so I thought.

While in Miami, I had many meetings arranged to talk with various modeling agencies interested in working with me. I'll never forget the meeting at Wilhelmina. It's etched in my brain, like a battle wound on a soldier freshly returned home from war. I was so nervous, sitting in the waiting room. It was ridiculous. I was a small-town girl, waiting to meet with one of the world's best modeling agencies. I was in a slight panic while waiting to be called back. The zebra-striped chairs and funky house music intimidated the hell out of me. All of these things were so new, so foreign to me.

Finally, the agent called us back. My mom led the way, and I followed like a scared puppy. They sat us down and asked us to wait while they retrieved my portfolio. As they retrieved my book of work, it seemed like my mom and I sat at the cold, oversized, round table for an eternity. It hit me. My intuition found its voice and came screaming from the inside out, "This is not right. This life… this job is not for me."

Tears fell from my face like a waterfall. They were tears of consequence, and I couldn't make it stop. I felt like I was about to throw up. My body was numb. I was afraid to disappoint my mom, but worse, something inside me was speaking that I knew I couldn't fight. It was something strong. I could feel its power and somehow knew it was divine and trustworthy. It was my intuition. Why it affected me like this, I wouldn't come to understand until almost twelve years later.

As we sat there waiting and the tears were flowing, I looked over at my mom, and without me even saying a word to her, she said, "I know, honey. Let's just sit through this meeting to respect their time. Then we'll go home."

Her words comforted me like a warm blanket and mended the divide in my heart. We finished the meeting, thanked them for their time, and left on the note that I had a lot to consider. Boy, did I ever! I was mad at myself for feeling this way and confused too. I had a contract with this amazing agency on the table, an offer to work with Revlon, and travel opportunities to Cape Town and Milan. They even had a place for me to live in a models' home with other well-known models. *Have I lost my mind?! What is wrong with me?* I thought.

And although those thoughts demanded my attention, my heart was louder, "Kim, this isn't you. You won't be happy. This isn't for you. Don't do it."

Even though I didn't understand what I was feeling, I somehow was still able to trust it. I always have. I told my mom I just wanted to pack it up and go home. She knew. A mother knows best, I guess. But she had to let me figure it out on my own. I had honored my intuition and my heart, and I was immediately rewarded. I had introverted back into my heart space, and everything that once felt invasive and threatening dissipated. My intuition used every avenue possible to speak my truth and express conflict—uncontrollable tears, upset stomach, rapid heartbeat, and sweaty palms, just to name a few.

The rest of my time in Miami was spent in the bathroom vomiting, as I purged the untruth I had encountered. It had actually made me that sick. The inner chaos taking place in my heart was manifesting physically, and I had no chance at resisting my heart. I surrendered right then and there. I stayed in the bathroom until it was time to leave. As I yielded to my heart, the symptoms dissolved, and I began to feel like myself again.

Looking back on this experience, I know it was not in my life plan, my purpose, to pursue modeling at that time in my life. I wasn't ready. I didn't know myself, and traveling the world seemed impossible in this state of mind. I was underdeveloped mentally, emotionally, and intuitively. I was afraid of the world literally because I hadn't connected to my inner world, my heart.

I've come to realize that, without a connection to the heart, life seems impossible to embrace, and a sense of purpose escapes you like a ghost in the night. One must passionately connect with the inner space, the heart. The connection must be felt authentically through passionate desire, not duty. The heart is the place of power, and this is where purpose will speak its truth to you. You must only quiet the mind to hear it.

To experience a life with purpose and feel purposeful in our day-to-day life, we must get to know ourselves on the soul level. Connection to our sacred inner space, yet again, proves its importance. If we maintain a deep connection to our inner selves and our heart, then a life with purpose and fulfillment will prevail. We gain a sense of knowing that no outside job or career is our purpose, but rather, the fact that we *exist* is our purpose. Sadly, as my guides mentioned, all too often though, we complicate it and can't accept the simplicity in that. Our existence is our purpose, and we utilize free will as an avenue for evolution.

Personally, I think our purpose has nothing to do with what we're doing physically. But I am talking from the perspective of a medium. We can't abandon the human side of ourselves, and we need to understand both sides of ourselves so we can maintain balance. I will explain purpose on the soul level first, and then we can talk about the physical level.

I've seen many people walk in the illusion of searching for their purpose in the external sense, basically looking for something they should be doing instead of being. From my perspective and with what my guides have taught me, our existence is our purpose.

It's as simple as that. We often overcomplicate it and overthink what this could possibly mean though, and in turn, we end up confused and lost. Free will is the bridge that closes the gap between soul purpose and physical purpose. I once heard a powerful phrase that said we should concentrate on being human *beings* instead of human *doings*. This is basically what I'm referring to. Your existence is your soul's purpose, to experience life and consciousness through your perspective. Free will determines how you experience and express that physically. We have again turned ourselves inside out thinking that what we are doing is more important than just being.

We have it backward. The aftermath is that, if we are not doing, we feel a lack of purpose instead of finding purpose in just being present. Again, it's the simplicity that we keep tripping over.

The collateral damage from that can be devastating and depressing. The more we externalize our search for purpose, the more we will feel purposeless. We lose ourselves within the search. The only thing that is true and guaranteed is God's affinity within us, so if our sense of purpose is understood there, it will always be fulfilled, but if it is dependent upon something external, it will always be dying and escaping you. The reason I say "dying" is because external things and circumstances change continually. But God's affinity within you is absolute and pure, unaffected and unbiased, and not based on anything external. It's our belief that our internal divinity can be influenced. That skews our relationship with the divine inside ourselves.

God is always expressing Himself in you and through you. You are a manifestation of the essence of God's love for the type of you and the who that you are, and merely to just reside in it exists in that love in everything you do. I think the most important thing to realize is that the mere fact you have life and breath in your lungs is your purpose, and through free will you express that however you choose. If we can silence the mind and hush the desire to engage with the thoughts, then our true self will naturally be realized. As we do this, we begin residency within our truest essence of ourselves. Bravery is required though, that is, bravery to detach from the memory, the emotions, and the knowledge that, for so long, we have identified ourselves with. If we attach ourselves to any of these things, we also are falling into the illusions that they create. The truest form of self exists outside of these things. You are not your emotions, your knowledge, or your memory. These are just experiences, subject to and confined to the physical, material world. Your essence is outside of all of those things. Trust yourself enough to get to know yourself in this quiet, blissful place. Throughout this process, we must uphold determination and humility to authentically become aware of ourselves, to awaken to ourselves.

So many of us are searching for what inspires us, sets our soul on fire, and gives us a sense of purpose. We must not forget to let ourselves *be* inspired rather than *search* for inspiration. And when we realize that purpose, that is our best opportunity to express God's essence within us. In this inside-out world, we are always searching for ourselves and what makes us different. What if we stop searching and attempt to exist in a place outside of and beyond all of the illusions that we think we are?

What do I mean? Well, take away your identity with your gender, race, name, religion, marital status, like/dislikes, childhood, job, how much money you have, family, heartbreaks, memories, hopes, and dreams. Take away those monumental experiences that shaped you into who you are today. Take away your identity with your lifestyle, hobbies, and groups of friends.

And so on. Take away everything from this human life you're experiencing. Now the most important part is to examine the leftovers. What's there? What do you feel in this beautiful, quiet space? This, my friend, is the space where the true essence of your being exists, and to think of the oxymoron, it's in the leftovers. Or do we have it all backward in where we've put our focus? Something to sit with for I while, I do believe.

God is the force that gives immortal existence to all living things. God is not segregated into certain cultures; nor is He confined to existing among only certain religious practice. You see, that limits God, and those are man-made ideations. God is limitless, without bounds. God's essence cannot be held within or contained within any parameters. And if we employ this belief, then we have only come to know a punitive God. The totality of all living things is God, yet God is in every individual thing too. Knowing this, we can easily realize there is life in everything and, because of that, purpose as well. Rest in having peace by knowing that God is always in you, and though you may neglect God, as we all have at times, God cannot neglect Himself, which is you. God is in you; therefore, He can never neglect you. What a comforting thing to realize. It is the essence of who you are. The more you recognize God in yourself, the more you'll experience God's love for you in life. God is continually expressing Himself as you through you. This is your purpose.

I do believe humans in general, in some cultures, have lost their adoration for human life though, and we rarely leave anything sacred anymore. Not all cultures but the popularity in what I'm addressing is growing. Some cultures have become overly generous in sharing negativity. It seems the general response to tragedy these days is to globalize local tragic events. Although we can sympathize with the victims and their families, we shouldn't blame all of mankind for an individual's actions or a local catastrophe. Sporadic, scattered events of evil and tragedy far too often are overidentified with as a whole, resulting in insult to all of mankind. In doing this, we lose hope and fall without purpose.

There are school shootings, robberies, and crimes that happen everywhere every day. One tragic event does not make all of mankind the same. One catastrophe does not mean God or Mother Nature is angry with us. We are equating the actions of an individual to collective worth of humankind. This is simply unrealistic. It's time we stop thinking that way. We are experiencing polarities of all levels of consciousness. This is nothing new. The

Bible even speaks of mass murders and catastrophe, but because we are technologically advanced, we share the negativity and perseverate on it. We even capitalize on it for far too long. If we choose to focus on the negativity, that's all we'll ever experience. There is just as much beauty, but we must be willing to see it too. When we allow our perspective to shift, a new sense of purpose is found.

Clearly people who take to crime to express themselves are operating at a much lower level of consciousness. And sadly, I have met many of these people who have not experienced God's grace inside of their own hearts. Nonetheless, acts of hate and crime aren't the answer, but saying that mankind is falling apart and deficient in love isn't the answer either.

I think, if we lose hope in mankind because of an individual's actions, then we have forgotten our own capabilities to make a beautiful life and even spread and share that beauty. We have defaulted to the outward reliance on pleasure and happiness instead of creating it within. We blame humankind for creating a world of hatred and negativity, yet we are the very source we blame for neglecting the power within. We can't point fingers if we haven't taken action to make the change we hope to see. My heart breaks for victims of such acts of violence and even the perpetrator in his delusional outcry, but I'll never blame humankind for an individual's actions.

Personally, I have seen too many acts of kindness and generosity; witnessed selflessness; and experienced miracles. I've been a giver and receiver of gratitude, love, and appreciation for me to say that our world is ugly. It's not. It's time we stop complaining and shift our focus to see what we are missing while focusing of the negative. There is beauty around every corner and in everything, but if our hearts aren't open to it, we won't see it and experience it. And a life without purpose prevails.

There is also illness everywhere and around every corner, from which we learn and grow. There is a lesson in everything. We just have to open our hearts to it. If there weren't, we'd have no room for growth or evolution. So remember, perhaps we shouldn't blame our society or mankind for one individual's actions. Perhaps we should search within for our personal capabilities to make a difference. This, I promise, will reveal life's purpose.

Your existence is your purpose. Focus on being, not doing.

Chapter 12

Barriers

The only barriers in life are the ones you accept. It's the belief in something as a hindrance that makes it a barrier. As a secular culture obsessed with certainty, we often create our own barriers through uncertainties. We acknowledge the uncertainties and give them life, therefore creating our own barriers. The only barriers we'll ever experience are the ones we've created and allowed. We almost would rather step out with certainty than through faith. In this, we've lost the ability to trust ourselves and our presence in the universe.

Trust your presence in the universe. You are an important part to the universal puzzle. The question isn't what you think you are, but what you believe you're not. That will always manifest barriers in your path. Abandon the need for certainty, and open the inner heart space. Allow trust within.

As a medium and spiritual coach, I've witnessed countless individuals who give more life to their fears instead of their hopes. In turn, they are creating a path of great resistance for themselves. Even worse is the mentality that people carry during the struggle, believing they deserve the difficulty, and they cling to it and overidentify with it. Further developing that reality, they stifle the possibility of change for themselves.

In example, I've had many clients book private sessions with me after suffering the loss of a pregnancy. Their hope for a future successful pregnancy becomes incarcerated by the past events and emotions tied to them. Fear of history repeating itself becomes their present state of emotional awareness. They begin to name all the potential barriers between them and their goal of a healthy pregnancy through fear and uncertainty, complicating things further. I remind you here, where thought goes, energy flows. And if thought fixates on barriers, they'll manifest.

Similarly, I've seen individuals so disillusioned by their fear and struggles that they don't know themselves outside of those fears. The self-awareness becomes confined and limited to conditions of suffering, and when asked to let go of that, anxiety arises. They become even more fearful and apprehensive because now what we are truly doing is laying down the ego, surrendering it all together. And as we do, we experience its death. It brings forth a sense of loss. The only thing dying though is the old you, the disillusioned you, the one that clings to false realities and divorces you from your true self. As we shed the ego, we naturally fall into the path of least resistance.

Most of us spend our lives avoiding the situations that have the highest potential to help us grow. When we allow ourselves to stay with uncertainty and discomfort, without trying to fix it, we connect with our inner selves and evolve.

To evolve, all that truly matters is if you have the belief. Do you truly believe in yourself? Your dreams? Your spirit? Can you surrender the barriers you've attached to? Life forces us to quickly dance through our days, and we don't often take time to slow down and align with our dreams. You have the power to manifest whatever you want and what you think about. Because you can dream it, you are the foundation uphold it.

Thought energy and emotional awareness are your two best tools for removing barriers in your life. That capability to manifest is intensified as you emotionally align with your thoughts and believe in the highest good for yourself. Manifest your dreams by aligning with the emotional reality of them. Surrender the attachments you've developed to self-created barriers, and release the burdens.

But if you doubt yourself in any way, you'll slowdown that manifestation. And the same applies for worry. If you prepare for misfortune, it will happen. If you worry that something awful will happen, your worry energy will help manifest it too. Your reality is a direct reflection of your energy, your thoughts, and your beliefs.

Look around you. Do you see it? How does this inspire you to make changes in your life? We fool ourselves by preparing and thinking we'll be ready when actually the preparations will manifest the difficulty. It is like saying to your spouse, "Honey, remind me to get toothpaste at the store." You've already told the universe that you'll forget, and now the backup plan will be needed.

Something to remember though in this process is to never underestimate the power of your dreams and the influence of your human spirit. The potential for greatness lives within each of us, and it's solely up to us to give life to it through that potential. The following is a channeled message from my guides about manifestation:

Manifestation is simple. Awareness must be allowed through consciousness to manifest anything. The word "allowed" is used intentionally here. It denotes a level of first believing and accepting what you're trying to manifest. Sit with this concept a moment. Oftentimes we work to manifest something in our lives without accepting it first. We must accept it in our hearts through belief in the highest good of all concerned that the manifestation is possible.

If you're trying to manifest more travel in your life, you should plant the seeds. Here is how you do that: vision and emotion. You must be able to visualize what you are trying to manifest. Visualize as many details as possible. What do the emotions feel like in this vision? Allow the details to come to you, but do not develop an attachment. If you always have an excuse like, "Yeah, but I really can't see that happening because A, B, and C," then you're not ready to manifest. Speak to the universe, and it will respond.

This, I've come to experience personally time and time again.

Plant the seeds. Begin telling the universe what you want. But realize that what you want already exists. You just have to merge your consciousness with the existence of it. This is where the emotion dynamic comes in. Visualizing something helps to merge with it, and emotional energy amplifies it. Once you put your energy into visualizing something, you are also putting your consciousness there through a level of awareness as a part of its existence. It's like telepathic travel, being deliberate with your thoughts to shift your reality. Where you put your thought energy, you also put your awareness through consciousness. The more the energy you put into it, the better your ability to bring it into your reality will be. But this can be like a double-edged sword. If you focus on negative, you'll manifest it.

Begin planting your thoughts and your energy where you want it to manifest. In example, if want to travel, plant your energy there on that topic. You can be specific but without attachments. Now bring in the emotion aspect. When you're trying to manifest and you plant your intentions, also plant your emotions. This is an important element for manifesting the best life for yourself. When you plant your thoughts and your intentions on traveling (using a beach, for example), also plant your emotions there. Connect to those emotions, and plant them. As you do, you are beginning to merge with that reality. Know that you are also creating the next phase of the manifestation process, nourishing the manifestation. But we'll get to that later.

For right now, I want you to focus on what I've already said. Manifestation occurs out of love and ego. With ego comes doubt, worry, fear, apprehension, and uncertainty. You must identify ego at its source and separate from it to manifest what you want. When you identify the fears and separate from them by letting go, you will live a more fulfilling life, letting go of worry and doubt. Focus on planting the seeds with vision and emotion to begin the manifestation process. Enjoy the feeling of letting go. Also identify your attachments, and be emotionally brave and honest with yourself. This will also help you manifest easier. The emotions and thoughts attached are important. The universe is very literal, so when you energetically nourish, be specific.

Let's go back to the example of traveling. If you're trying to manifest travel, you've already put the vision and emotion to it. Now it's time to nourish it. You do that through devotion. If you continue the energy flow, the manifestation will occur sooner. Think about it like this. If you plant an apple seed, you wouldn't just water it once and expect it to grow into a large fruit-bearing tree. You have to keep at it. Manifestation is similar. Continue sending emotions and vision to the seed you planted.

In this process, as mentioned, don't give way to doubt. That comes from ego. This is getting into the meat of it. Your ego wants to have a say in everything you do. Your ego is going to get loud and try to make you doubt, and ask, "Well, what if this happens?" or "I'm not sure about that." Ego chatter is going to try to have a place in the process all along the way. It's part of being human. It's your job to identify it. Doubt, fear, and worry in

175

any form comes from ego. In releasing any fear, doubt, or worry, this is energetically fostering the growth of your manifestation.

Again, the universe is very literal. You can't manifest your dreams on a someday note. The universe doesn't understand what someday means. Someday has no definition, no existence. And if you subject your dreams to existing someday, they'll never come to pass.

You (hopefully) have already been putting thought energy into that which you are trying to manifest, and as you do that, you are helping yourself align with the reality of it. And that's the next part of full-on manifestation. So much goes into it. Here is a list of helpful tips. Then we'll go deeper.

- *Leave fear/worry/doubt far behind.*
- *Give gratitude, knowing it's in the works.*
- *Don't limit yourself. Release attachments.*
- *Get ready. Prepare for the manifestation.*

Okay, first, as you release fear, worry, and doubt, you are aligning with the truth of what you want to manifest. You wouldn't want to align with fear, so don't let it be a part of this process. You have not been given a reason to fear. Fear will make the manifestation a negatively skewed version of what you really want. Now as you let go of any doubt or worry, give gratitude for your manifestation. It raises your vibration to match you and place you into that reality. If you are giving thanks for it, you are aligning with the reality of it. People often get caught up in their self-imposed limitations. The only limits you have are the ones you accept. Let your imagination grow the picture of your manifestation.

Lastly, begin to prepare. Prepare yourself for this manifestation. When you prepare in whatever way it is, again you are aligning with and bringing the manifestation into your reality.

Our capacity to engage with vulnerability is the direct pathway to our inner space. If we don't allow ourselves to move into his place of peace, we begin to live like savages, perpetuating our barriers in life. Vulnerability releases the grip of anything external on you, and allows change. We must accept change. As we do, we cancel out everything that was previously seen as a barrier. If we don't do anything different, we won't experience anything new. Adaptability is the key trait to allow ourselves to do so.

We must honor our true self without shame. We are created in love and should love ourselves without limits. Don't let your visions, goals, and dreams be ruled and determined by someone else's fears, for that's his or her limitations, not yours. And if your dreams and aspirations are altered to comfort another, then you haven't connected with your passion yet. Don't deny yourself of your truth because of others' inabilities to accept or understand. Love them in their ignorance. Love them in the place of adversity. But don't let them become your barrier.

You were born free. Be brave. Step out into the light, and don't conform to external standards and settle in unhappiness. You are unique. You are one of a kind. No other energetic vibration can create another you. Everything you want is waiting for you on the other side of fear. Don't let fear be a barrier any longer. You've heard it said before. Life awaits you on the other side of your fears. Sit in silence with yourself. Listen to your heart. Follow your heart, and you'll never fail.

Labels are limiting and even mummifying to your ability to express yourself. We get so wrapped up in achieving or chasing labels that we forget why we're chasing them in the first place. Then we create attachments, overidentify with labels, and lose sight of who we are. We abandon the capacity to see ourselves as anything different. Egocentric addictions to labels are the catalyst of divided consciousness.

Labels do make communication easier at times, but all too often, I've seen people overidentify with certain labels. This overidentification process, I believe, is the true reason for stagnancy. Individuals identify and often overidentify with a label and then become disillusioned and stagnant.

Deep emotional capacity is required for one to reflect inward. Take an honest look at yourself and identify the labels you are attached to. And then, through bravery and self-trust, release them. The same capacity is required for us to know ourselves, outside of all the labels, titles, and stereotypes.

Sometimes we even cling to different labels and identify ourselves with them because that's what society wants or is encouraging. But at this point, it should be no secret that doing so is divorcing yourself from the true essence of who and what you are. You are essentially robbing yourself of you. That is it. Being you should be the easiest thing in the world, but if upholding a label makes it hard, make a change. Surrender.

The only barriers in life are the ones you accept.

Chapter 13

Motivation

Show up for yourself each and every day! Work hard, and be in love with your work so that, when you look back and reflect, you make yourself proud. Only you can be you and get the job done. Stop and ponder how amazing that is for a moment. There is no other you out there. No other vibrational frequency exists like you. When you stop to think about it, it is mind-blowing to realize. Almost overwhelming really that God took the time and energy to make you, create you, and give you life. Stand in your power and claim it. Align with the inner space. That is the true essence of who you are, that sense of self that no one else can touch. And boldly be you.

It is so important to align with your inner self every day so you can connect with your personal power and, in that, realize your motivation. I say "realize" here because it's not something external to find, but rather, something internal to awaken to. It's always been here. It's just a matter of you shifting your awareness to it to make the conscious connection. As you begin to realign internally with your personal power, you'll notice your capacity to trust yourself will evolve as well. As you develop your awareness internally and remove the conditioned layers of the ego, internal motivation then naturally abides.

All of life's circumstances will beckon for our attention, and if we are willing to listen with positive intent, we can transmute any and every circumstance into a lesson to grow from. We must challenge ourselves though to look beyond our own expectations, doubts, and fears and allow the universe to motivate us too. The universe needs you and is calling you to fill in the missing piece of its puzzle. You are needed. That is why you exist. Feel that connection through your heart, and as you answer the call, trust that you are needed.

A mind-bending message came through from my guides recently that I'll share, "You are not your thoughts, but you are what you think you are." So be mindful of what you think about yourself, but mostly show up, and make yourself proud. I share this because I've seen so many people react to their thoughts and assume things that aren't true, and in turn, their reactive thoughts become their motivations. When his happens, you can almost always guarantee negative experiences to follow.

Motivation comes from within, in realizing the God essence in us all, and if we stay connected to our hearts, we'll stay connected to our personal motivation and drive too. This is another area where we often turn ourselves inside out. We allow our motivations to be externally rooted, and if they are, eventually that source of motivation will run out of energy to supply you. I've seen it happen many times, and when individuals externally cultivate motivation, the drive eventually dissolves.

Ask yourself these questions to see if you too are externally dependent for motivation: Do you often start projects with great intensity and a lot of motivation and then quickly become uninterested? Once you start something, do you lose interest upon realizing it's not what you thought it'd be? If you answered yes, then perhaps your motivations are externally rooted and quickly dissolve with time.

If there is change in something, there is life in it. Transformation gives life to all forms, and all forms with life will experience transformation. Motivation for our actions can be unknown, and

I have often witnessed the pain one can experience through this. This is the demonstration of lack of conscious connection to the inner self. If motivation for change comes through pain associated with the past or anxieties tied to the future, then that pain will only continue. Fear then becomes the motivating factor at hand. If we act on our fear and allow ourselves to be motivated by it, the motivation won't last long because it is not coming from a true source. So again, be mindful of where your motivation is coming from. Further, as you connect to the present moment and your inner self in the present moment, the existence of your motivation will never need fed. Motivation naturally abides in the authentic state of awareness.

For example, I met with a young father once. He was going through a divorce, and he was spending a lot of precious time taking videos and photographs of his children, in fear that his wife would one day take them from him after the divorce. My guides reminded him that fear was motivating him. By allowing that fearful motivation to grab hold of him, he was helping those circumstances to manifest in his life.

All too often I've seen people become motivated by their past or future. They carry the fear of history repeating itself or apprehensions of the worst-case scenario playing out in the future. Fear becomes the vessel for the motivation to exist, and since fear itself comes from ego, it perpetually creates one illusion after another.

As humans, we experience a variety of intense emotions that can often become our strongest motivators in life. Fear of rejection or the past repeating itself is some of the strongest motivators I've seen in many actions. If negativity is our motivating factor, we will only experience more of the same.

If the heart and the mind are continually employed through contemplation, then we'll allow ourselves the inner space required for inspiration and growth. But if that inner space is always occupied with fear and anxiety, inspiration and motivation will seem to be nowhere in sight. It becomes a feeling of having exhausted all personal resources. There must be an intimate relationship between the heart and open space within that allows inspiration, for that's the birthplace of motivation. We must *allow* ourselves to be inspired rather than *seek* the inspiration.

The difference is, as we allow, we are giving life to that open sacred heart space within us all, that place where nirvana is experienced. This requires us to break free from the ball and chains that keeps us dependent on the external world and to realize that we are always becoming. We are forward-moving energetic patterns with life force with consciousness, always unraveling in our beauty and continually becoming our greatest. As we stumble into this realization, the motivation naturally grows within us. Even through the hardest of time, the byway for personal growth and development comes from looking at the silver lining. If we turn away from the silver lining and choose not to grow from it, we begin to live like savages among a "me" culture.

We carry the weight of the world on our shoulders when we have no direction and no motivation. Most commonly, this is when we turn ourselves inside out, yet again, for purpose and motivation, giving away our power. Keep your power. Don't turn yourself inside out. You'll never get to know yourself that way.

Perhaps it's the bigger picture enriching our lives with experiences that have value to us as soul investments. I think this also carries over into the relationships and bonds that we create and maintain throughout life. To me, those are also soul investments. The soul growth that we promote for ourselves through outside relationships is dynamic and valuable.

Whether pain, sorrow, joy, or contentment, every situation we encounter will sprout its own emotions, and it's up to us to listen to those emotions. Pain and sorrow foster appreciation while joy can nurture new growth, but all of these are useless without our attention through the lens of positivity. I encourage you to listen the emotions you are feeling and be brave enough to ask yourself why you're feeling them. The truth just might set you free.

Fear of the uncertain is to blame here. It forces us to be vulnerable, and sadly, too many of us cling to our ego rather than allow vulnerability. Personally I think allowing vulnerability means allowing God to show His grace in our lives. Vulnerability is the intersection that joins our hearts with God. But at times, we turn to the false security of our ego and deny ourselves the opportunity to be present with God. To allow vulnerability is to fall into the divine and allow God's grace to take over. This is where strength is born. It takes strength within one's self to let go of our ego and need for control, that is, to be vulnerable. Through trusting this process, we grow in our strength and connection with God. From one moment to the next, there is always an in-between space, and that's the very space where we let God in, the space in which vulnerability exists.

So remember, God has spoken unto you, and that is the very essence of who you are. Your every breath is watched over, your every action is known, your sadness brings wisdom, your pain is a chance for strength, and your fear is the perfect place for renewal. It's up to you to allow that renewal in.

When we lose motivation, we carry the weight of the world

on our shoulders. Be still, and let the world inspire you.

Chapter 14

Heartbeat

When you go with the flow of life, you align with the heartbeat of the universe. You align with the rhythm of all that is. Allow that rhythm to flow through you, inspire you, and influence that way you spread hope and love through the world. As you align with the flow of the universe, within every action you take is new heartbeat and new passion. That heartbeat, carried by your passion, perpetuates the cycles of life. And then, when you dance to the rhythm of that heartbeat, you become an instrument for the universe.

Let the universe and all its wonders sing through you. As you do, unity among the world is increased because of you. Everything you think, say, and do has momentum and collaterally affects everything else. You and every action from you creates a ripple effect that speaks to the entire universe. No action will go without reaction, even if that response occurs across the world. And when love is the language you're speaking to the universe, you raise your own vibration and create unity among the collective consciousness of the world.

We're all connected, and what better way to realize this than simply laying under the stars at night. We all sleep under the same stars and rise to the same sun. When we can acknowledge the unity that this creates, which we all reside in, we'll then be able to see through the illusion of separateness that our minds create. The tragedy in believing in separateness is that, when we do, we're creating an arrhythmia in the heartbeat of the universe.

My absolute favorite song lyric beautifully demonstrates the unity I'm talking about. The diversity of this lyric is why I love it so much. It can be interpreted many ways, but in the end, it still creates unity, no matter the interpretation. "When you find, your way up to the stars, I hope you find, we aint that far apart." This lyric from Kip Moore in his song "Lil Mamma" inspired me in ways I only hope I can articulate. To me, this simply means, when we can surrender to something bigger than ourselves and open our hearts, we'll be connected again. We're not that far apart ever in race, ethnicity, spirituality, religion, tradition, beliefs, and so on. We're all searching for the same thing, peace through hope.

These differences only create separateness if we allow ourselves to view them that way. If we believe in and cling to our perception of separateness, then that's what we'll experience. Our heads get in the way of our hearts and convince us that we're far apart. We must forgive ourselves of our own ego and others too so we can find our way up to the stars and find each other again and unite.

You see, in this life, this universe, there is truly only one heartbeat, one rhythm that embodies all of life, everything in existence, and gives life to every other living thing, God. I often use the word *love* interchangeably with *God*, and I will here too. Love gives life, a heartbeat to anything and everything we do.

An interesting story I watched on TV demonstrated this beautiful connection to the heartbeat of the universe I speak of. Like Americans, Guatemalans often visit cemeteries to honor and remember their loved ones. While there in a Guatemalan cemetery, you are likely to find individuals flying kites over the graveyard while standing atop some of the tombstones of their loved ones.

You see, Guatemalans believe that, when flying a kite at the cemetery to honor their loved ones, the spirit of their family or friend will provide the winds and guide the flight of the kite. They are the gateway between heaven and earth, and the flight of the kite represents the soaring of the spirit of their loved one. So you'll see many of them constructing unique kites with ornate designs and beautifully woven colors to honor their deceased loved ones. As I was watching this, the symbolism and gesture captivated me. What a beautiful way to honor your departed loved ones.

The passion we put into the things we do creates a new heartbeat in synch with the universe. This heartbeat pushes us forward through times of grief and despair, the heartbeat that intertwines our joy with the warmth of the sun, the heartbeat that allows the melody of our favorite song to touch our soul and give us hope, the heartbeat that provides salvation from our fears and carries us to a moment of strength. The heartbeat is within the soldier's love for his country and creates laughter between best friends. The heartbeat is in the passion between two lovers. The heartbeat is in the photo taken by the passionate photographer and in the golden lyrics produced by the songwriter. This heartbeat is the love affair between an author and his or her writing. The heartbeat uses the artist to create a masterpiece and the nurturing mother to care for her young children. That unifying heartbeat is everywhere and in everything. We must allow ourselves to become harmoniously involved with that universal heartbeat.

Far too often, it is omitted during our cold, dark days. We abandon our own heartbeat in moments of despair and pain. Hopelessness takes over in our hearts and crowds the intimate connection to our heart. We're left feeling defeated. As this happens and passion escapes us, another heartbeat comes to an end, and we fall back into a familiar place, a place of despair and grief.

Although we lose sight of God within us, He cannot possibly lose sight of us. So we must remind ourselves perhaps to surrender to the stars, to something greater than ourselves, and find salvation in the heartbeat of the universe. That heartbeat will continue its nurturing rhythm and will be ready to pick us back up right where we left off when we're ready.

We always choose the emotions we are experiencing. Then we employ them, give them life, and create our reality through them. Always remember, your pain is never in vain, never worthless or useless. It's the very vessel for your resurrection to that divine, unwavering heartbeat within you that connects you to the universe. The sacred inner place is the intersection where your heart meets God's grace. Keep your mind employed by wonder, and foster the connection to the heartbeat of the universe, God, and the essence of all that is. We are all one, and the heart beats to the rhythm of oneness among us all. It's always there, waiting with open arms to welcome you back.

Lay down your fears and resurrect your hopes. Let go of your nonvirtuous thoughts, and allow yourself to accept your greatness. God is the life force in us all, the essence of every living, breathing thing. To me, the word *God* means existence because, without God, there is no existence. Because of this, everything is perfect and is, as it is supposed to be. God is the heartbeat in everything, the reason why there is passion in or for anything. And even when we've abandoned our own heartbeat, it's still there, waiting for us the moment we surrender our ego. God is always waiting for us at the very place we gave up, became hopeless, or abandoned our self-worth. When our awareness takes residency in God's affinity within our hearts, we essentially are honoring our divine selves.

God's presence dwells in the spaces in between our thoughts, in between our emotions.

The essence of God cannot be embodied in any label, any type, or anything other than love. Although we try with such descriptions as pure, beautiful, absolute, light, love, and divine, these descriptions are only mere fractals of God's greatness, I do believe. The best of these, in my earthly opinion, is love. Love is a word that is good, not wants good. It is a word that describes existence, not action. But anything that happens in love can be described by it and assumes its natural position in the heartbeat that creates the universe. I think it can easily be said that, wherever there is passion, there also is the heartbeat of the universe. The heartbeat is the unwavering rhythm of God's love in everything.

Let your actions be kind and in harmony with the world inside you and around you. Let the universe sing through you. Let your actions be virtuous, your speech be soft, and your thoughts always rebirth you into a place of love and light.

God is the heartbeat, the passion in everything. Surrender your fears, and

resurrect your dreams as you come to know God's affinity within you.

Made in the USA
San Bernardino, CA
16 June 2017